C-3505   CAREER EXAMINATION SERIES

This is your
PASSBOOK for...

Beginning Clerical Worker

Test Preparation Study Guide
Questions & Answers

NATIONAL LEARNING CORPORATION®

COPYRIGHT NOTICE

This book is SOLELY intended for, is sold ONLY to, and its use is RESTRICTED to individual, bona fide applicants or candidates who qualify by virtue of having seriously filed applications for appropriate license, certificate, professional and/or promotional advancement, higher school matriculation, scholarship, or other legitimate requirements of education and/or governmental authorities.

This book is NOT intended for use, class instruction, tutoring, training, duplication, copying, reprinting, excerption, or adaptation, etc., by:

1) Other publishers
2) Proprietors and/or Instructors of "Coaching" and/or Preparatory Courses
3) Personnel and/or Training Divisions of commercial, industrial, and governmental organizations
4) Schools, colleges, or universities and/or their departments and staffs, including teachers and other personnel
5) Testing Agencies or Bureaus
6) Study groups which seek by the purchase of a single volume to copy and/or duplicate and/or adapt this material for use by the group as a whole without having purchased individual volumes for each of the members of the group
7) Et al.

Such persons would be in violation of appropriate Federal and State statutes.

PROVISION OF LICENSING AGREEMENTS – Recognized educational, commercial, industrial, and governmental institutions and organizations, and others legitimately engaged in educational pursuits, including training, testing, and measurement activities, may address request for a licensing agreement to the copyright owners, who will determine whether, and under what conditions, including fees and charges, the materials in this book may be used them. In other words, a licensing facility exists for the legitimate use of the material in this book on other than an individual basis. However, it is asseverated and affirmed here that the material in this book CANNOT be used without the receipt of the express permission of such a licensing agreement from the Publishers. Inquiries re licensing should be addressed to the company, attention rights and permissions department.

All rights reserved, including the right of reproduction in whole or in part, in any form or by any means, electronic or mechanical, including photocopying, recording, or by any information storage and retrieval system, without permission in writing from the Publisher.

Copyright © 2024 by
National Learning Corporation

212 Michael Drive, Syosset, NY 11791
(516) 921-8888 • www.passbooks.com
E-mail: info@passbooks.com

PASSBOOK® SERIES

THE *PASSBOOK® SERIES* has been created to prepare applicants and candidates for the ultimate academic battlefield – the examination room.

At some time in our lives, each and every one of us may be required to take an examination – for validation, matriculation, admission, qualification, registration, certification, or licensure.

Based on the assumption that every applicant or candidate has met the basic formal educational standards, has taken the required number of courses, and read the necessary texts, the *PASSBOOK® SERIES* furnishes the one special preparation which may assure passing with confidence, instead of failing with insecurity. Examination questions – together with answers – are furnished as the basic vehicle for study so that the mysteries of the examination and its compounding difficulties may be eliminated or diminished by a sure method.

This book is meant to help you pass your examination provided that you qualify and are serious in your objective.

The entire field is reviewed through the huge store of content information which is succinctly presented through a provocative and challenging approach – the question-and-answer method.

A climate of success is established by furnishing the correct answers at the end of each test.

You soon learn to recognize types of questions, forms of questions, and patterns of questioning. You may even begin to anticipate expected outcomes.

You perceive that many questions are repeated or adapted so that you can gain acute insights, which may enable you to score many sure points.

You learn how to confront new questions, or types of questions, and to attack them confidently and work out the correct answers.

You note objectives and emphases, and recognize pitfalls and dangers, so that you may make positive educational adjustments.

Moreover, you are kept fully informed in relation to new concepts, methods, practices, and directions in the field.

You discover that you are actually taking the examination all the time: you are preparing for the examination by "taking" an examination, not by reading extraneous and/or supererogatory textbooks.

In short, this PASSBOOK®, used directedly, should be an important factor in helping you to pass your test.

BEGINNING CLERICAL WORKER

DUTIES

As a <u>CLERK I</u>, you would process forms, screen documents, maintain files and keep records. You would have a supervisor in this job. Your duties might include compiling information; preparing forms and documents and sending them out; answering questions orally or in writing; looking up information. You might do any of these or other related duties.

As a <u>STORES CLERK I</u>, you would receive, store and distribute goods, equipment, material or records. You would work under a supervisor in a stockroom, warehouse, records center, institution retail store or commissary. Your duties might include receiving and checking shipments of material; keeping records; issuing supplies or stock; packaging goods for shipment or storage; loading and unloading equipment or furniture; operating a retail store or commissary; coding and disposing of batches of records and files.

As a <u>CALCULATIONS CLERK I</u>, you would do mathematical computations and handle numerical records. You would work under the direct supervision of a higher-level clerk or a program manager. Your duties might include maintaining statistical or financial records; preparing numerical reports (including charts and graphs); compiling data from various sources; handling computer files; answering questions about transactions and procedures.

As a <u>MAIL AND SUPPLY CLERK</u>, you would process mail and handle office supplies and equipment. Your duties might include sorting and delivering mail; receiving, storing, distributing office supplies; unloading shipments; keeping an inventory of forms and publications; operating equipment such as sorters, collators, inserters, duplicating and postage machines.

As a <u>CLOTHING CLERK</u>, you would work in state institutions receiving, distributing and storing items like clothing, dry goods and bedding. You might also repair or keep records of items received or distributed.

SCOPE OF THE EXAMINATION

The written test will be designed to test for knowledge, skills, and/or abilities in such areas as:
1. Name and number checking;
2. Coding information;
3. Clerical operations with letters and numbers;
4. Filing;
5. Arithmetic computations;
6. Arithmetic reasoning;
7. Keeping simple inventory records;. and
8. Reading.

HOW TO TAKE A TEST

I. YOU MUST PASS AN EXAMINATION

A. *WHAT EVERY CANDIDATE SHOULD KNOW*

Examination applicants often ask us for help in preparing for the written test. What can I study in advance? What kinds of questions will be asked? How will the test be given? How will the papers be graded?

As an applicant for a civil service examination, you may be wondering about some of these things. Our purpose here is to suggest effective methods of advance study and to describe civil service examinations.

Your chances for success on this examination can be increased if you know how to prepare. Those "pre-examination jitters" can be reduced if you know what to expect. You can even experience an adventure in good citizenship if you know why civil service exams are given.

B. *WHY ARE CIVIL SERVICE EXAMINATIONS GIVEN?*

Civil service examinations are important to you in two ways. As a citizen, you want public jobs filled by employees who know how to do their work. As a job seeker, you want a fair chance to compete for that job on an equal footing with other candidates. The best-known means of accomplishing this two-fold goal is the competitive examination.

Exams are widely publicized throughout the nation. They may be administered for jobs in federal, state, city, municipal, town or village governments or agencies.

Any citizen may apply, with some limitations, such as the age or residence of applicants. Your experience and education may be reviewed to see whether you meet the requirements for the particular examination. When these requirements exist, they are reasonable and applied consistently to all applicants. Thus, a competitive examination may cause you some uneasiness now, but it is your privilege and safeguard.

C. *HOW ARE CIVIL SERVICE EXAMS DEVELOPED?*

Examinations are carefully written by trained technicians who are specialists in the field known as "psychological measurement," in consultation with recognized authorities in the field of work that the test will cover. These experts recommend the subject matter areas or skills to be tested; only those knowledges or skills important to your success on the job are included. The most reliable books and source materials available are used as references. Together, the experts and technicians judge the difficulty level of the questions.

Test technicians know how to phrase questions so that the problem is clearly stated. Their ethics do not permit "trick" or "catch" questions. Questions may have been tried out on sample groups, or subjected to statistical analysis, to determine their usefulness.

Written tests are often used in combination with performance tests, ratings of training and experience, and oral interviews. All of these measures combine to form the best-known means of finding the right person for the right job.

II. HOW TO PASS THE WRITTEN TEST

A. NATURE OF THE EXAMINATION

To prepare intelligently for civil service examinations, you should know how they differ from school examinations you have taken. In school you were assigned certain definite pages to read or subjects to cover. The examination questions were quite detailed and usually emphasized memory. Civil service exams, on the other hand, try to discover your present ability to perform the duties of a position, plus your potentiality to learn these duties. In other words, a civil service exam attempts to predict how successful you will be. Questions cover such a broad area that they cannot be as minute and detailed as school exam questions.

In the public service similar kinds of work, or positions, are grouped together in one "class." This process is known as *position-classification*. All the positions in a class are paid according to the salary range for that class. One class title covers all of these positions, and they are all tested by the same examination.

B. FOUR BASIC STEPS

1) Study the announcement

How, then, can you know what subjects to study? Our best answer is: "Learn as much as possible about the class of positions for which you've applied." The exam will test the knowledge, skills and abilities needed to do the work.

Your most valuable source of information about the position you want is the official exam announcement. This announcement lists the training and experience qualifications. Check these standards and apply only if you come reasonably close to meeting them.

The brief description of the position in the examination announcement offers some clues to the subjects which will be tested. Think about the job itself. Review the duties in your mind. Can you perform them, or are there some in which you are rusty? Fill in the blank spots in your preparation.

Many jurisdictions preview the written test in the exam announcement by including a section called "Knowledge and Abilities Required," "Scope of the Examination," or some similar heading. Here you will find out specifically what fields will be tested.

2) Review your own background

Once you learn in general what the position is all about, and what you need to know to do the work, ask yourself which subjects you already know fairly well and which need improvement. You may wonder whether to concentrate on improving your strong areas or on building some background in your fields of weakness. When the announcement has specified "some knowledge" or "considerable knowledge," or has used adjectives like "beginning principles of…" or "advanced … methods," you can get a clue as to the number and difficulty of questions to be asked in any given field. More questions, and hence broader coverage, would be included for those subjects which are more important in the work. Now weigh your strengths and weaknesses against the job requirements and prepare accordingly.

3) Determine the level of the position

Another way to tell how intensively you should prepare is to understand the level of the job for which you are applying. Is it the entering level? In other words, is this the position in which beginners in a field of work are hired? Or is it an intermediate or advanced level? Sometimes this is indicated by such words as "Junior" or "Senior" in the class title. Other jurisdictions use Roman numerals to designate the level – Clerk I, Clerk II, for example. The word "Supervisor" sometimes appears in the title. If the level is not indicated by the title, check the description of duties. Will you be working under very close supervision, or will you have responsibility for independent decisions in this work?

4) Choose appropriate study materials

Now that you know the subjects to be examined and the relative amount of each subject to be covered, you can choose suitable study materials. For beginning level jobs, or even advanced ones, if you have a pronounced weakness in some aspect of your training, read a modern, standard textbook in that field. Be sure it is up to date and has general coverage. Such books are normally available at your library, and the librarian will be glad to help you locate one. For entry-level positions, questions of appropriate difficulty are chosen – neither highly advanced questions, nor those too simple. Such questions require careful thought but not advanced training.

If the position for which you are applying is technical or advanced, you will read more advanced, specialized material. If you are already familiar with the basic principles of your field, elementary textbooks would waste your time. Concentrate on advanced textbooks and technical periodicals. Think through the concepts and review difficult problems in your field.

These are all general sources. You can get more ideas on your own initiative, following these leads. For example, training manuals and publications of the government agency which employs workers in your field can be useful, particularly for technical and professional positions. A letter or visit to the government department involved may result in more specific study suggestions, and certainly will provide you with a more definite idea of the exact nature of the position you are seeking.

III. KINDS OF TESTS

Tests are used for purposes other than measuring knowledge and ability to perform specified duties. For some positions, it is equally important to test ability to make adjustments to new situations or to profit from training. In others, basic mental abilities not dependent on information are essential. Questions which test these things may not appear as pertinent to the duties of the position as those which test for knowledge and information. Yet they are often highly important parts of a fair examination. For very general questions, it is almost impossible to help you direct your study efforts. What we can do is to point out some of the more common of these general abilities needed in public service positions and describe some typical questions.

1) General information

Broad, general information has been found useful for predicting job success in some kinds of work. This is tested in a variety of ways, from vocabulary lists to questions about current events. Basic background in some field of work, such as sociology or economics, may be sampled in a group of questions. Often these are principles which have become familiar to most persons through exposure rather than through formal training. It is difficult to advise you how to study for these questions; being alert to the world around you is our best suggestion.

2) Verbal ability

An example of an ability needed in many positions is verbal or language ability. Verbal ability is, in brief, the ability to use and understand words. Vocabulary and grammar tests are typical measures of this ability. Reading comprehension or paragraph interpretation questions are common in many kinds of civil service tests. You are given a paragraph of written material and asked to find its central meaning.

3) **Numerical ability**

Number skills can be tested by the familiar arithmetic problem, by checking paired lists of numbers to see which are alike and which are different, or by interpreting charts and graphs. In the latter test, a graph may be printed in the test booklet which you are asked to use as the basis for answering questions.

4) **Observation**

A popular test for law-enforcement positions is the observation test. A picture is shown to you for several minutes, then taken away. Questions about the picture test your ability to observe both details and larger elements.

5) **Following directions**

In many positions in the public service, the employee must be able to carry out written instructions dependably and accurately. You may be given a chart with several columns, each column listing a variety of information. The questions require you to carry out directions involving the information given in the chart.

6) **Skills and aptitudes**

Performance tests effectively measure some manual skills and aptitudes. When the skill is one in which you are trained, such as typing or shorthand, you can practice. These tests are often very much like those given in business school or high school courses. For many of the other skills and aptitudes, however, no short-time preparation can be made. Skills and abilities natural to you or that you have developed throughout your lifetime are being tested.

Many of the general questions just described provide all the data needed to answer the questions and ask you to use your reasoning ability to find the answers. Your best preparation for these tests, as well as for tests of facts and ideas, is to be at your physical and mental best. You, no doubt, have your own methods of getting into an exam-taking mood and keeping "in shape." The next section lists some ideas on this subject.

IV. KINDS OF QUESTIONS

Only rarely is the "essay" question, which you answer in narrative form, used in civil service tests. Civil service tests are usually of the short-answer type. Full instructions for answering these questions will be given to you at the examination. But in case this is your first experience with short-answer questions and separate answer sheets, here is what you need to know:

1) Multiple-choice Questions

Most popular of the short-answer questions is the "multiple choice" or "best answer" question. It can be used, for example, to test for factual knowledge, ability to solve problems or judgment in meeting situations found at work.

A multiple-choice question is normally one of three types—

- It can begin with an incomplete statement followed by several possible endings. You are to find the one ending which *best* completes the statement, although some of the others may not be entirely wrong.
- It can also be a complete statement in the form of a question which is answered by choosing one of the statements listed.

- It can be in the form of a problem – again you select the best answer.

Here is an example of a multiple-choice question with a discussion which should give you some clues as to the method for choosing the right answer:

When an employee has a complaint about his assignment, the action which will *best* help him overcome his difficulty is to
- A. discuss his difficulty with his coworkers
- B. take the problem to the head of the organization
- C. take the problem to the person who gave him the assignment
- D. say nothing to anyone about his complaint

In answering this question, you should study each of the choices to find which is best. Consider choice "A" – Certainly an employee may discuss his complaint with fellow employees, but no change or improvement can result, and the complaint remains unresolved. Choice "B" is a poor choice since the head of the organization probably does not know what assignment you have been given, and taking your problem to him is known as "going over the head" of the supervisor. The supervisor, or person who made the assignment, is the person who can clarify it or correct any injustice. Choice "C" is, therefore, correct. To say nothing, as in choice "D," is unwise. Supervisors have and interest in knowing the problems employees are facing, and the employee is seeking a solution to his problem.

2) True/False Questions

The "true/false" or "right/wrong" form of question is sometimes used. Here a complete statement is given. Your job is to decide whether the statement is right or wrong.

SAMPLE: A roaming cell-phone call to a nearby city costs less than a non-roaming call to a distant city.

This statement is wrong, or false, since roaming calls are more expensive.

This is not a complete list of all possible question forms, although most of the others are variations of these common types. You will always get complete directions for answering questions. Be sure you understand *how* to mark your answers – ask questions until you do.

V. RECORDING YOUR ANSWERS

Computer terminals are used more and more today for many different kinds of exams.

For an examination with very few applicants, you may be told to record your answers in the test booklet itself. Separate answer sheets are much more common. If this separate answer sheet is to be scored by machine – and this is often the case – it is highly important that you mark your answers correctly in order to get credit.

An electronic scoring machine is often used in civil service offices because of the speed with which papers can be scored. Machine-scored answer sheets must be marked with a pencil, which will be given to you. This pencil has a high graphite content which responds to the electronic scoring machine. As a matter of fact, stray dots may register as answers, so do not let your pencil rest on the answer sheet while you are pondering the correct answer. Also, if your pencil lead breaks or is otherwise defective, ask for another.

Since the answer sheet will be dropped in a slot in the scoring machine, be careful not to bend the corners or get the paper crumpled.

The answer sheet normally has five vertical columns of numbers, with 30 numbers to a column. These numbers correspond to the question numbers in your test booklet. After each number, going across the page are four or five pairs of dotted lines. These short dotted lines have small letters or numbers above them. The first two pairs may also have a "T" or "F" above the letters. This indicates that the first two pairs only are to be used if the questions are of the true-false type. If the questions are multiple choice, disregard the "T" and "F" and pay attention only to the small letters or numbers.

Answer your questions in the manner of the sample that follows:

32. The largest city in the United States is
    A. Washington, D.C.
    B. New York City
    C. Chicago
    D. Detroit
    E. San Francisco

1) Choose the answer you think is best. (New York City is the largest, so "B" is correct.)
2) Find the row of dotted lines numbered the same as the question you are answering. (Find row number 32)
3) Find the pair of dotted lines corresponding to the answer. (Find the pair of lines under the mark "B.")
4) Make a solid black mark between the dotted lines.

VI. BEFORE THE TEST

Common sense will help you find procedures to follow to get ready for an examination. Too many of us, however, overlook these sensible measures. Indeed, nervousness and fatigue have been found to be the most serious reasons why applicants fail to do their best on civil service tests. Here is a list of reminders:

- Begin your preparation early – Don't wait until the last minute to go scurrying around for books and materials or to find out what the position is all about.
- Prepare continuously – An hour a night for a week is better than an all-night cram session. This has been definitely established. What is more, a night a week for a month will return better dividends than crowding your study into a shorter period of time.
- Locate the place of the exam – You have been sent a notice telling you when and where to report for the examination. If the location is in a different town or otherwise unfamiliar to you, it would be well to inquire the best route and learn something about the building.
- Relax the night before the test – Allow your mind to rest. Do not study at all that night. Plan some mild recreation or diversion; then go to bed early and get a good night's sleep.
- Get up early enough to make a leisurely trip to the place for the test – This way unforeseen events, traffic snarls, unfamiliar buildings, etc. will not upset you.
- Dress comfortably – A written test is not a fashion show. You will be known by number and not by name, so wear something comfortable.

- Leave excess paraphernalia at home – Shopping bags and odd bundles will get in your way. You need bring only the items mentioned in the official notice you received; usually everything you need is provided. Do not bring reference books to the exam. They will only confuse those last minutes and be taken away from you when in the test room.
- Arrive somewhat ahead of time – If because of transportation schedules you must get there very early, bring a newspaper or magazine to take your mind off yourself while waiting.
- Locate the examination room – When you have found the proper room, you will be directed to the seat or part of the room where you will sit. Sometimes you are given a sheet of instructions to read while you are waiting. Do not fill out any forms until you are told to do so; just read them and be prepared.
- Relax and prepare to listen to the instructions
- If you have any physical problem that may keep you from doing your best, be sure to tell the test administrator. If you are sick or in poor health, you really cannot do your best on the exam. You can come back and take the test some other time.

VII. AT THE TEST

The day of the test is here and you have the test booklet in your hand. The temptation to get going is very strong. Caution! There is more to success than knowing the right answers. You must know how to identify your papers and understand variations in the type of short-answer question used in this particular examination. Follow these suggestions for maximum results from your efforts:

1) Cooperate with the monitor

The test administrator has a duty to create a situation in which you can be as much at ease as possible. He will give instructions, tell you when to begin, check to see that you are marking your answer sheet correctly, and so on. He is not there to guard you, although he will see that your competitors do not take unfair advantage. He wants to help you do your best.

2) Listen to all instructions

Don't jump the gun! Wait until you understand all directions. In most civil service tests you get more time than you need to answer the questions. So don't be in a hurry. Read each word of instructions until you clearly understand the meaning. Study the examples, listen to all announcements and follow directions. Ask questions if you do not understand what to do.

3) Identify your papers

Civil service exams are usually identified by number only. You will be assigned a number; you must not put your name on your test papers. Be sure to copy your number correctly. Since more than one exam may be given, copy your exact examination title.

4) Plan your time

Unless you are told that a test is a "speed" or "rate of work" test, speed itself is usually not important. Time enough to answer all the questions will be provided, but this does not mean that you have all day. An overall time limit has been set. Divide the total time (in minutes) by the number of questions to determine the approximate time you have for each question.

5) Do not linger over difficult questions

If you come across a difficult question, mark it with a paper clip (useful to have along) and come back to it when you have been through the booklet. One caution if you do this – be sure to skip a number on your answer sheet as well. Check often to be sure that you have not lost your place and that you are marking in the row numbered the same as the question you are answering.

6) Read the questions

Be sure you know what the question asks! Many capable people are unsuccessful because they failed to *read* the questions correctly.

7) Answer all questions

Unless you have been instructed that a penalty will be deducted for incorrect answers, it is better to guess than to omit a question.

8) Speed tests

It is often better NOT to guess on speed tests. It has been found that on timed tests people are tempted to spend the last few seconds before time is called in marking answers at random – without even reading them – in the hope of picking up a few extra points. To discourage this practice, the instructions may warn you that your score will be "corrected" for guessing. That is, a penalty will be applied. The incorrect answers will be deducted from the correct ones, or some other penalty formula will be used.

9) Review your answers

If you finish before time is called, go back to the questions you guessed or omitted to give them further thought. Review other answers if you have time.

10) Return your test materials

If you are ready to leave before others have finished or time is called, take ALL your materials to the monitor and leave quietly. Never take any test material with you. The monitor can discover whose papers are not complete, and taking a test booklet may be grounds for disqualification.

VIII. EXAMINATION TECHNIQUES

1) Read the general instructions carefully. These are usually printed on the first page of the exam booklet. As a rule, these instructions refer to the timing of the examination; the fact that you should not start work until the signal and must stop work at a signal, etc. If there are any *special* instructions, such as a choice of questions to be answered, make sure that you note this instruction carefully.

2) When you are ready to start work on the examination, that is as soon as the signal has been given, read the instructions to each question booklet, underline any key words or phrases, such as *least, best, outline, describe* and the like. In this way you will tend to answer as requested rather than discover on reviewing your paper that you *listed without describing*, that you selected the *worst* choice rather than the *best* choice, etc.

3) If the examination is of the objective or multiple-choice type – that is, each question will also give a series of possible answers: A, B, C or D, and you are called upon to select the best answer and write the letter next to that answer on your answer paper – it is advisable to start answering each question in turn. There may be anywhere from 50 to 100 such questions in the three or four hours allotted and you can see how much time would be taken if you read through all the questions before beginning to answer any. Furthermore, if you come across a question or group of questions which you know would be difficult to answer, it would undoubtedly affect your handling of all the other questions.

4) If the examination is of the essay type and contains but a few questions, it is a moot point as to whether you should read all the questions before starting to answer any one. Of course, if you are given a choice – say five out of seven and the like – then it is essential to read all the questions so you can eliminate the two that are most difficult. If, however, you are asked to answer all the questions, there may be danger in trying to answer the easiest one first because you may find that you will spend too much time on it. The best technique is to answer the first question, then proceed to the second, etc.

5) Time your answers. Before the exam begins, write down the time it started, then add the time allowed for the examination and write down the time it must be completed, then divide the time available somewhat as follows:
    - If 3-1/2 hours are allowed, that would be 210 minutes. If you have 80 objective-type questions, that would be an average of 2-1/2 minutes per question. Allow yourself no more than 2 minutes per question, or a total of 160 minutes, which will permit about 50 minutes to review.
    - If for the time allotment of 210 minutes there are 7 essay questions to answer, that would average about 30 minutes a question. Give yourself only 25 minutes per question so that you have about 35 minutes to review.

6) The most important instruction is to *read each question* and make sure you know what is wanted. The second most important instruction is to *time yourself properly* so that you answer every question. The third most important instruction is to *answer every question*. Guess if you have to but include something for each question. Remember that you will receive no credit for a blank and will probably receive some credit if you write something in answer to an essay question. If you guess a letter – say "B" for a multiple-choice question – you may have guessed right. If you leave a blank as an answer to a multiple-choice question, the examiners may respect your feelings but it will not add a point to your score. Some exams may penalize you for wrong answers, so in such cases *only*, you may not want to guess unless you have some basis for your answer.

7) Suggestions
   a. Objective-type questions
      1. Examine the question booklet for proper sequence of pages and questions
      2. Read all instructions carefully
      3. Skip any question which seems too difficult; return to it after all other questions have been answered
      4. Apportion your time properly; do not spend too much time on any single question or group of questions

5. Note and underline key words – *all, most, fewest, least, best, worst, same, opposite,* etc.
6. Pay particular attention to negatives
7. Note unusual option, e.g., unduly long, short, complex, different or similar in content to the body of the question
8. Observe the use of "hedging" words – *probably, may, most likely,* etc.
9. Make sure that your answer is put next to the same number as the question
10. Do not second-guess unless you have good reason to believe the second answer is definitely more correct
11. Cross out original answer if you decide another answer is more accurate; do not erase until you are ready to hand your paper in
12. Answer all questions; guess unless instructed otherwise
13. Leave time for review

b. Essay questions
1. Read each question carefully
2. Determine exactly what is wanted. Underline key words or phrases.
3. Decide on outline or paragraph answer
4. Include many different points and elements unless asked to develop any one or two points or elements
5. Show impartiality by giving pros and cons unless directed to select one side only
6. Make and write down any assumptions you find necessary to answer the questions
7. Watch your English, grammar, punctuation and choice of words
8. Time your answers; don't crowd material

8) Answering the essay question

Most essay questions can be answered by framing the specific response around several key words or ideas. Here are a few such key words or ideas:

M's: manpower, materials, methods, money, management
P's: purpose, program, policy, plan, procedure, practice, problems, pitfalls, personnel, public relations

a. Six basic steps in handling problems:
1. Preliminary plan and background development
2. Collect information, data and facts
3. Analyze and interpret information, data and facts
4. Analyze and develop solutions as well as make recommendations
5. Prepare report and sell recommendations
6. Install recommendations and follow up effectiveness

b. Pitfalls to avoid
1. *Taking things for granted* – A statement of the situation does not necessarily imply that each of the elements is necessarily true; for example, a complaint may be invalid and biased so that all that can be taken for granted is that a complaint has been registered

2. *Considering only one side of a situation* – Wherever possible, indicate several alternatives and then point out the reasons you selected the best one
3. *Failing to indicate follow up* – Whenever your answer indicates action on your part, make certain that you will take proper follow-up action to see how successful your recommendations, procedures or actions turn out to be
4. *Taking too long in answering any single question* – Remember to time your answers properly

IX. AFTER THE TEST

Scoring procedures differ in detail among civil service jurisdictions although the general principles are the same. Whether the papers are hand-scored or graded by machine we have described, they are nearly always graded by number. That is, the person who marks the paper knows only the number – never the name – of the applicant. Not until all the papers have been graded will they be matched with names. If other tests, such as training and experience or oral interview ratings have been given, scores will be combined. Different parts of the examination usually have different weights. For example, the written test might count 60 percent of the final grade, and a rating of training and experience 40 percent. In many jurisdictions, veterans will have a certain number of points added to their grades.

After the final grade has been determined, the names are placed in grade order and an eligible list is established. There are various methods for resolving ties between those who get the same final grade – probably the most common is to place first the name of the person whose application was received first. Job offers are made from the eligible list in the order the names appear on it. You will be notified of your grade and your rank as soon as all these computations have been made. This will be done as rapidly as possible.

People who are found to meet the requirements in the announcement are called "eligibles." Their names are put on a list of eligible candidates. An eligible's chances of getting a job depend on how high he stands on this list and how fast agencies are filling jobs from the list.

When a job is to be filled from a list of eligibles, the agency asks for the names of people on the list of eligibles for that job. When the civil service commission receives this request, it sends to the agency the names of the three people highest on this list. Or, if the job to be filled has specialized requirements, the office sends the agency the names of the top three persons who meet these requirements from the general list.

The appointing officer makes a choice from among the three people whose names were sent to him. If the selected person accepts the appointment, the names of the others are put back on the list to be considered for future openings.

That is the rule in hiring from all kinds of eligible lists, whether they are for typist, carpenter, chemist, or something else. For every vacancy, the appointing officer has his choice of any one of the top three eligibles on the list. This explains why the person whose name is on top of the list sometimes does not get an appointment when some of the persons lower on the list do. If the appointing officer chooses the second or third eligible, the No. 1 eligible does not get a job at once, but stays on the list until he is appointed or the list is terminated.

X. HOW TO PASS THE INTERVIEW TEST

The examination for which you applied requires an oral interview test. You have already taken the written test and you are now being called for the interview test – the final part of the formal examination.

You may think that it is not possible to prepare for an interview test and that there are no procedures to follow during an interview. Our purpose is to point out some things you can do in advance that will help you and some good rules to follow and pitfalls to avoid while you are being interviewed.

What is an interview supposed to test?

The written examination is designed to test the technical knowledge and competence of the candidate; the oral is designed to evaluate intangible qualities, not readily measured otherwise, and to establish a list showing the relative fitness of each candidate – as measured against his competitors – for the position sought. Scoring is not on the basis of "right" and "wrong," but on a sliding scale of values ranging from "not passable" to "outstanding." As a matter of fact, it is possible to achieve a relatively low score without a single "incorrect" answer because of evident weakness in the qualities being measured.

Occasionally, an examination may consist entirely of an oral test – either an individual or a group oral. In such cases, information is sought concerning the technical knowledges and abilities of the candidate, since there has been no written examination for this purpose. More commonly, however, an oral test is used to supplement a written examination.

Who conducts interviews?

The composition of oral boards varies among different jurisdictions. In nearly all, a representative of the personnel department serves as chairman. One of the members of the board may be a representative of the department in which the candidate would work. In some cases, "outside experts" are used, and, frequently, a businessman or some other representative of the general public is asked to serve. Labor and management or other special groups may be represented. The aim is to secure the services of experts in the appropriate field.

However the board is composed, it is a good idea (and not at all improper or unethical) to ascertain in advance of the interview who the members are and what groups they represent. When you are introduced to them, you will have some idea of their backgrounds and interests, and at least you will not stutter and stammer over their names.

What should be done before the interview?

While knowledge about the board members is useful and takes some of the surprise element out of the interview, there is other preparation which is more substantive. It *is* possible to prepare for an oral interview – in several ways:

1) Keep a copy of your application and review it carefully before the interview

This may be the only document before the oral board, and the starting point of the interview. Know what education and experience you have listed there, and the sequence and dates of all of it. Sometimes the board will ask you to review the highlights of your experience for them; you should not have to hem and haw doing it.

2) Study the class specification and the examination announcement

Usually, the oral board has one or both of these to guide them. The qualities, characteristics or knowledges required by the position sought are stated in these documents. They offer valuable clues as to the nature of the oral interview. For example, if the job involves supervisory responsibilities, the announcement will usually indicate that knowledge of modern supervisory methods and the qualifications of the candidate as a supervisor will be tested. If so, you can expect such questions, frequently in the form of a hypothetical situation which you are expected to solve. NEVER go into an oral without knowledge of the duties and responsibilities of the job you seek.

3) Think through each qualification required

Try to visualize the kind of questions you would ask if you were a board member. How well could you answer them? Try especially to appraise your own knowledge and background in each area, *measured against the job sought*, and identify any areas in which you are weak. Be critical and realistic – do not flatter yourself.

4) Do some general reading in areas in which you feel you may be weak

For example, if the job involves supervision and your past experience has NOT, some general reading in supervisory methods and practices, particularly in the field of human relations, might be useful. Do NOT study agency procedures or detailed manuals. The oral board will be testing your understanding and capacity, not your memory.

5) Get a good night's sleep and watch your general health and mental attitude

You will want a clear head at the interview. Take care of a cold or any other minor ailment, and of course, no hangovers.

What should be done on the day of the interview?

Now comes the day of the interview itself. Give yourself plenty of time to get there. Plan to arrive somewhat ahead of the scheduled time, particularly if your appointment is in the fore part of the day. If a previous candidate fails to appear, the board might be ready for you a bit early. By early afternoon an oral board is almost invariably behind schedule if there are many candidates, and you may have to wait. Take along a book or magazine to read, or your application to review, but leave any extraneous material in the waiting room when you go in for your interview. In any event, relax and compose yourself.

The matter of dress is important. The board is forming impressions about you – from your experience, your manners, your attitude, and your appearance. Give your personal appearance careful attention. Dress your best, but not your flashiest. Choose conservative, appropriate clothing, and be sure it is immaculate. This is a business interview, and your appearance should indicate that you regard it as such. Besides, being well groomed and properly dressed will help boost your confidence.

Sooner or later, someone will call your name and escort you into the interview room. *This is it*. From here on you are on your own. It is too late for any more preparation. But remember, you asked for this opportunity to prove your fitness, and you are here because your request was granted.

What happens when you go in?

The usual sequence of events will be as follows: The clerk (who is often the board stenographer) will introduce you to the chairman of the oral board, who will introduce you to the other members of the board. Acknowledge the introductions before you sit down. Do not be surprised if you find a microphone facing you or a stenotypist sitting by. Oral interviews are usually recorded in the event of an appeal or other review.

Usually the chairman of the board will open the interview by reviewing the highlights of your education and work experience from your application – primarily for the benefit of the other members of the board, as well as to get the material into the record. Do not interrupt or comment unless there is an error or significant misinterpretation; if that is the case, do not hesitate. But do not quibble about insignificant matters. Also, he will usually ask you some question about your education, experience or your present job – partly to get you to start talking and to establish the interviewing "rapport." He may start the actual questioning, or turn it over to one of the other members. Frequently, each member undertakes the questioning on a particular area, one in which he is perhaps most competent, so you can expect each member to participate in the examination. Because time is limited, you may also expect some rather abrupt switches in the direction the questioning takes, so do not be upset by it. Normally, a board member will not pursue a single line of questioning unless he discovers a particular strength or weakness.

After each member has participated, the chairman will usually ask whether any member has any further questions, then will ask you if you have anything you wish to add. Unless you are expecting this question, it may floor you. Worse, it may start you off on an extended, extemporaneous speech. The board is not usually seeking more information. The question is principally to offer you a last opportunity to present further qualifications or to indicate that you have nothing to add. So, if you feel that a significant qualification or characteristic has been overlooked, it is proper to point it out in a sentence or so. Do not compliment the board on the thoroughness of their examination – they have been sketchy, and you know it. If you wish, merely say, "No thank you, I have nothing further to add." This is a point where you can "talk yourself out" of a good impression or fail to present an important bit of information. Remember, *you close the interview yourself*.

The chairman will then say, "That is all, Mr. _____, thank you." Do not be startled; the interview is over, and quicker than you think. Thank him, gather your belongings and take your leave. Save your sigh of relief for the other side of the door.

How to put your best foot forward

Throughout this entire process, you may feel that the board individually and collectively is trying to pierce your defenses, seek out your hidden weaknesses and embarrass and confuse you. Actually, this is not true. They are obliged to make an appraisal of your qualifications for the job you are seeking, and they want to see you in your best light. Remember, they must interview all candidates and a non-cooperative candidate may become a failure in spite of their best efforts to bring out his qualifications. Here are 15 suggestions that will help you:

1) Be natural – Keep your attitude confident, not cocky

If you are not confident that you can do the job, do not expect the board to be. Do not apologize for your weaknesses, try to bring out your strong points. The board is interested in a positive, not negative, presentation. Cockiness will antagonize any board member and make him wonder if you are covering up a weakness by a false show of strength.

2) Get comfortable, but don't lounge or sprawl

Sit erectly but not stiffly. A careless posture may lead the board to conclude that you are careless in other things, or at least that you are not impressed by the importance of the occasion. Either conclusion is natural, even if incorrect. Do not fuss with your clothing, a pencil or an ashtray. Your hands may occasionally be useful to emphasize a point; do not let them become a point of distraction.

3) Do not wisecrack or make small talk

This is a serious situation, and your attitude should show that you consider it as such. Further, the time of the board is limited – they do not want to waste it, and neither should you.

4) Do not exaggerate your experience or abilities

In the first place, from information in the application or other interviews and sources, the board may know more about you than you think. Secondly, you probably will not get away with it. An experienced board is rather adept at spotting such a situation, so do not take the chance.

5) If you know a board member, do not make a point of it, yet do not hide it

Certainly you are not fooling him, and probably not the other members of the board. Do not try to take advantage of your acquaintanceship – it will probably do you little good.

6) Do not dominate the interview

Let the board do that. They will give you the clues – do not assume that you have to do all the talking. Realize that the board has a number of questions to ask you, and do not try to take up all the interview time by showing off your extensive knowledge of the answer to the first one.

7) Be attentive

You only have 20 minutes or so, and you should keep your attention at its sharpest throughout. When a member is addressing a problem or question to you, give him your undivided attention. Address your reply principally to him, but do not exclude the other board members.

8) Do not interrupt

A board member may be stating a problem for you to analyze. He will ask you a question when the time comes. Let him state the problem, and wait for the question.

9) Make sure you understand the question

Do not try to answer until you are sure what the question is. If it is not clear, restate it in your own words or ask the board member to clarify it for you. However, do not haggle about minor elements.

10) Reply promptly but not hastily

A common entry on oral board rating sheets is "candidate responded readily," or "candidate hesitated in replies." Respond as promptly and quickly as you can, but do not jump to a hasty, ill-considered answer.

11) Do not be peremptory in your answers

A brief answer is proper – but do not fire your answer back. That is a losing game from your point of view. The board member can probably ask questions much faster than you can answer them.

12) Do not try to create the answer you think the board member wants

He is interested in what kind of mind you have and how it works – not in playing games. Furthermore, he can usually spot this practice and will actually grade you down on it.

13) Do not switch sides in your reply merely to agree with a board member

Frequently, a member will take a contrary position merely to draw you out and to see if you are willing and able to defend your point of view. Do not start a debate, yet do not surrender a good position. If a position is worth taking, it is worth defending.

14) Do not be afraid to admit an error in judgment if you are shown to be wrong

The board knows that you are forced to reply without any opportunity for careful consideration. Your answer may be demonstrably wrong. If so, admit it and get on with the interview.

15) Do not dwell at length on your present job

The opening question may relate to your present assignment. Answer the question but do not go into an extended discussion. You are being examined for a *new* job, not your present one. As a matter of fact, try to phrase ALL your answers in terms of the job for which you are being examined.

Basis of Rating

Probably you will forget most of these "do's" and "don'ts" when you walk into the oral interview room. Even remembering them all will not ensure you a passing grade. Perhaps you did not have the qualifications in the first place. But remembering them will help you to put your best foot forward, without treading on the toes of the board members.

Rumor and popular opinion to the contrary notwithstanding, an oral board wants you to make the best appearance possible. They know you are under pressure – but they also want to see how you respond to it as a guide to what your reaction would be under the pressures of the job you seek. They will be influenced by the degree of poise you display, the personal traits you show and the manner in which you respond.

ABOUT THIS BOOK

This book contains tests divided into Examination Sections. Go through each test, answering every question in the margin. We have also attached a sample answer sheet at the back of the book that can be removed and used. At the end of each test look at the answer key and check your answers. On the ones you got wrong, look at the right answer choice and learn. Do not fill in the answers first. Do not memorize the questions and answers, but understand the answer and principles involved. On your test, the questions will likely be different from the samples. Questions are changed and new ones added. If you understand these past questions you should have success with any changes that arise. Tests may consist of several types of questions. We have additional books on each subject should more study be advisable or necessary for you. Finally, the more you study, the better prepared you will be. This book is intended to be the last thing you study before you walk into the examination room. Prior study of relevant texts is also recommended. NLC publishes some of these in our Fundamental Series. Knowledge and good sense are important factors in passing your exam. Good luck also helps. So now study this Passbook, absorb the material contained within and take that knowledge into the examination. Then do your best to pass that exam.

EXAMINATION SECTION

EXAMINATION SECTION
TEST 1

DIRECTIONS: Each question or incomplete statement is followed by several suggested answers or completions. Select the one that BEST answers the question or completes the statement. *PRINT THE LETTER OF THE CORRECT ANSWER IN THE SPACE AT THE RIGHT.*

Questions 1-4.

DIRECTIONS: Questions 1 through 4 are to be answered using only the information in the following passage.

Planning for storage layout in terms of the supplies to be stored involves the intelligent and realistic application of a stockman's basic resources - space. The main objective of storage planning is the maximum use of available space. The planning and layout of space are dependent upon the types of supplies expected to be stored, and certain characteristics must be considered. Some supplies must be protected from dampness, extreme changes of temperature, and other such conditions. Iron and steel products rust quickly at high temperatures with high humidity. High temperatures also cause some plastics to melt and change shape, while extreme dampness can cause paper to mildew and wood to warp. Hazardous articles, including flammable items like paint and rubber cement, should be stored separated from each other and from other types of supplies.

Extremes in characteristics such as size, shape, and weight need to be considered in laying out space. Large, awkward containers and unusually heavy items generally should be stored near doors with aisles leading directly to them and/or shipping and receiving facilities. Light and fragile items cannot be stacked to a height which would cause crushing or other damage to containers and contents. Fast-moving articles should be stored in locations from which they can be handled quickly and efficiently.

1. It is MOST important to store articles like paints and rubber cement in areas where
    A. they can be protected from theft
    B. shipping and receiving doors are easily accessible
    C. they can be isolated from other supplies
    D. boxes containing them can be stacked as high as possible

2. Storage locations from which items can be selected and issued quickly are recommended for supplies classified as
    A. fragile
    B. fast-moving
    C. under-sized
    D. flammable

3. In order to prevent supplies made of iron from rusting, they should be stored in areas with _____ humidity and _____ temperature.
    A. low; high
    B. low; low
    C. high; high
    D. high; low

4. Which of the following characteristics is NOT considered in the above passage on storage planning and layout?
    The _____ of the item to be stored.
    A. size
    B. quantity
    C. weight
    D. shape

Questions 5-12.

DIRECTIONS: Each of Questions 5 through 12 consists of a word in capitals followed by four suggested meanings of the word. For each question, choose the meaning which you think is BEST and print the letter of the correct answer in the space at the right.

5. CATALOG
   A. to list   B. to rate   C. to print   D. to price

6. DURABLE
   A. smooth   B. sticky   C. lasting   D. feeling

7. MUTUAL
   A. silent   B. shared   C. changing   D. broken

8. REJECT
   A. rewrite   B. refuse   C. release   D. regret

9. OBSTRUCT
   A. teach   B. darken   C. block   D. resist

10. CORRODE
    A. melt   B. rust   C. burn   D. warp

11. EXCESS
    A. surplus   B. storage   C. spacing   D. survey

12. FLEXIBLE
    A. neatly folded   B. easily broken
    C. easily bent   D. neatly piled

Questions 13-16.

DIRECTIONS: Questions 13 through 16 are to be answered using ONLY the information in the following passage.

The "active stock" portion of the inventory is that portion which is kept for the purpose of satisfying the shop's expected requirements of that material. It is directly related to the "order quantity." The "order quantity" is found by determining the expected annual requirements of the shop and dividing this by the number of orders for this merchandise which will be placed during the year. The most economical number of orders is usually found by considering the cost of ordering and storing inventory.

The "safety stock" portion of the inventory is that portion which is created to take care of above-average or unexpected demands on the inventory. This portion is directly related to the point at which the order is placed. The amount of safety stock is not determined by com-

paring order costs and carrying costs, but on the need for protection against stock shortages for each stock item under consideration. Some stock items will need more safety stock than others, depending upon how much difference there has been in the past between the expected usage of material and the actual amount needed and used for any given time period, plus the reliability of the suppliers' delivery and of the order lead-time. If the expected usage of an item has always been 100% accurately predicted, then theoretically there would be no need for "safety stock."

13. According to the above passage, the *active stock* inventory is that portion of the inventory which is

    A. used most frequently by management
    B. ordered on a regular basis, such as every month
    C. expected to meet the organization's anticipated inventory needs
    D. needed to protect against shortages in very active inventory items

14. According to the above passage, what factors must be considered to determine the order quantity for any active stock item?

    A. Anticipated requirements, ordering cost, and cost of storing inventory
    B. Order lead-time and delivery service
    C. Variety of stock items ordered in the previous year
    D. The largest quantity ever ordered

15. Maintaining a safety stock portion of the inventory is

    A. *good,* because it provides for unexpected demands on the inventory
    B. *good,* because it makes the inventory more valuable than it actually is
    C. *poor,* because it provides unnecessary work for stockmen since the Inventory is rarely used
    D. *poor,* because it makes storage areas overcrowded and unsafe

16. The above passage indicates that 100 percent accuracy in forecasting future activity will eliminate the need for

    A. reliable deliveries
    B. active stock
    C. safety stock
    D. deviation in total order quantity

17. At the start of a certain month, you have 185 jars of glue in stock. During that month, you fill the following orders: 3 orders for 12 jars each, 2 orders for 10 jars each, 2 orders for 8 jars each, one order for 9 jars, one order for 20 jars, and one order for 24 jars.
    If you received no shipments of glue during that month, the number of jars of glue you will have on hand at the end of the month is

    A. 60 B. 77 C. 102 D. 125

18. Assume that you are ordering merchandise from a vendor who gives a discount of 10%, plus an additional 2% for payment within 30 days.
    If, on October 21st, you order merchandise which has a catalogue value of $714, and the bill is paid by November 10th, the net amount of the payment should be MOST NEARLY

    A. $628.32 B. $629.95 C. $630.74 D. $632.60

19. Suppose that there are 293 people in your shop and 11% of them are women. The number of men in your shop is

   A. 261   B. 263   C. 269   D. 271

20. In March, Department Z made an overpayment of $34.26 to the Superior Fuel Oil Company. This amount was credited to the Department's account. In April, the fuel bill amounted to $378.12.
   Considering the credit on the Department's account, the payment that should be remitted for the April fuel bill is

   A. $343.86   B. $343.96   C. $344.86   D. $344.96

21. A certain agency ordered and used 1,020 one-pound balls of twine last year at a total cost of $357.
   If the price per ball of twine remained constant throughout the year, the cost of each one-pound ball was

   A. 25¢   B. 30¢   C. 35¢   D. 40¢

22. You place an order at the Abbey Office Supply Company for three of each of the following items: metal desk at $129 each; chair at $65 each; desk lamp at $24 each.
   If this supply company gives a 15% discount on all orders totaling $500 or more, the net price of this order is

   A. $567.90   B. $555.90   C. $484.20   D. $479.20

23. Suppose that there are 27 people in your department and your boss tells you that he is putting on an extra laborer and two mechanics.
   The percent of the increase in personnel for your department would be MOST NEARLY

   A. 8%   B. 9%   C. 10%   D. 11%

Questions 24-29.

DIRECTIONS:

CODE TABLE

Code Letter	b	d	f	a	g	s	z	w	h	u
Code Number	1	2	3	4	5	6	7	8	9	0

In the Code Table above, each code letter has a corresponding code number directly beneath it.

Each of Questions 24 through 29 contains three sets of code letters and code numbers. In each set, the code numbers should correspond with the code letters as given in the table, but there is a coding error in some of the sets. Examine the sets in each question carefully.

Mark your answer:
   A if there is a coding error in only ONE of the sets in the question;
   B if there is a coding error in any TWO of the sets in the question;
   C if there is a coding error in all THREE sets in the question;
   D if there is a coding error in NONE of the sets in the question.

SAMPLE QUESTION:

   fgzduwaf - 35720843
   uabsdgfw - 04262538
   hhfaudgs - 99340257

In the sample question above, the first set is right because each code number matches the code letter as in the Code Table. In the second set, the corresponding number for the code letter b is wrong because it should be 1 instead of 2. In the third set, the corresponding number for the last code letter s is wrong because it should be 6 instead of 7. Since there is an error in two of the sets, the answer to the above sample question is B.

24. fsbughwz - 36104987
    zwubgasz - 78025467
    ghgufddb - 59583221   24._____

25. hafgdaas - 94351446
    ddsfabsd - 22734162
    wgdbssgf - 85216553   25._____

26. abfbssbd - 41316712
    ghzfaubs - 59734017
    sdbzfwza - 62173874   26._____

27. whfbdzag - 89412745
    daaszuub - 24467001
    uzhfwssd - 07936623   27._____

28. zbadgbuh - 71425109
    dzadbbsz - 27421167
    gazhwaff - 54798433   28._____

29. fbfuadsh - 31304265
    gzfuwzsb - 57300671
    bashhgag - 14699535   29._____

Questions 30-35.

DIRECTIONS: Questions 30 through 35 are to be answered on the basis of the information in the Weekly Requisition Form below.

WEEKLY REQUISITION FORM

Storehouse 17	Date 7.17	Dept. Code 809	Dept. Budget Code 13942	Dept. Requisition No. 1029	
Deliver to: Requisition Dept. Atlantic Hospital			Unit and/or Division Kitchen	Address 66 W. Highland Blvd.	
Storehouse Item Code	Description Incl. Size, Number or Measurements		Unit of Issue	No. Units Requested	Unit Price	Tot. Cost
895	Chocolate Syrup #10 can		case	5	7.35	
1926	Mayonnaise 1 gal. jar		case	2	6.73	13.46
1945	Black pepper, ground 1.lb. can		lb	3		1.89
1976	34 fresh eggs			7	.41	2.87
220	Pineapple, crushed #10 can		case	4	5.89	23.56
5395	Straws 8 1/2" long 500 to box		box	12	.47	5.64
452	Applesauce 4 1/2 oz. jar 24/case		case		1.65	6.60
Requested By John Smith	Title Shop Clerk	Material Issued By _____ Date _____ Total No. Pieces _____		Material Received By Signed _____ Date _____ Total No. Pieces _____		
Approved By	Supervisor					

30. What is the total cost of the chocolate syrup order described in the requisition form above?

    A. $36.75   B. $34.35   C. $31.65   D. $30.15

31. The week of 7/24, the price of a gallon jar of mayonnaise increased by 4 cents. If there are 6 gallon jars of mayonnaise per case, how much is the total cost of the mayonnaise order for the week of 7/24, if the order quantity is the same as the previous week?

    A. $6.97   B. $7.21   C. $13.68   D. $13.94

32. What is the unit price for ground black pepper as described in the requisition form above?

    A. 36¢   B. 43¢   C. 57¢   D. 63¢

33. Based on the information provided in the requisition form above, what is the correct unit of issue for fresh eggs?

    A. Each   B. Container   C. Dozen   D. Case

34. There are 6 #10 cans of crushed pineapple per case. Based on the information in the requisition form above, how many #10 cans of pineapple are being ordered?

    A. 16   B. 20   C. 24   D. 30

35. Each week the cook at Atlantic Hospital uses 84 4 1/2 ounce jars of applesauce. Based on the requisition for the week of 7/17, how many cases must be ordered to fill the need for the following week (7/24) in order to avoid storing an excess supply of applesauce? (Assume that there was no excess from the week previous to 7/17.)

    A. 1 B. 2 C. 3 D. 4

36. Suppose that the shop in which you worked received 421 pieces of mail in one month, of which 64 were requests for information.
    The percent of letters which were requests for information is MOST NEARLY

    A. 13.2% B. 15.2% C. 15.5% D. 16.1%

37. The following is the year's stock issue record of cans of oil distributed for use in Agency Y: January - 107; February - 94; March - 113; April - 118; May - 122; June - 87; July - 89; August - 98; September - 110; October - 101; November - 105; December - 106.
    The monthly average of cans of oil distributed is MOST NEARLY

    A. 100 B. 102 C. 104 D. 106

38. Two trucks, A and B, are carrying stock from a warehouse to the shop. The weight of the truck alone is the tare; the weight of the loaded truck is the gross weight. Truck A has a tare of 4,637 pounds, and a gross weight of 6,955 pounds. Truck B has a tare of 4,489 pounds, and a gross weight of 6,723 pounds.
    What is the total weight of the loads of both trucks?
    _____ pounds.

    A. 3,452 B. 3,564 C. 4,552 D. 4,653

39. A stock carton measures 24" long, 18" wide, and 24" high. What is the maximum number of boxes measuring 4 1/2" long, 3" wide, and 3" high that can be packed inside the carton?

    A. 135 B. 256 C. 405 D. 432

40. If a ream of paper weighs 11 ounces, 36 reams of paper will weigh _____ pounds, _____ ounces.

    A. 22; 8 B. 24; 12 C. 33; 0 D. 39; 6

KEY (CORRECT ANSWERS)

1. C	11. A	21. C	31. D
2. B	12. C	22. B	32. D
3. B	13. C	23. D	33. C
4. B	14. A	24. C	34. C
5. A	15. A	25. C	35. C
6. C	16. C	26. B	36. B
7. B	17. A	27. B	37. C
8. B	18. A	28. D	38. C
9. C	19. A	29. C	39. B
10. B	20. A	30. A	40. B

TEST 2

DIRECTIONS: Each question or incomplete statement is followed by several suggested answers or completions. Select the one that BEST answers the question or completes the statement. *PRINT THE LETTER OF THE CORRECT ANSWER IN THE SPACE AT THE RIGHT.*

Questions 1-6.

DIRECTIONS: Questions 1 through 6 are to be answered on the basis of the information below.

A certain shop keeps an informational card file for all suppliers and merchandise. On each card is the supplier's name, the contract number for the merchandise he supplies, and a delivery date for the merchandise. In this filing system, the supplier's name is filed alphabetically, the contract number for the merchandise is filed numerically, and the delivery date is filed chronologically.

In Questions 1 through 6, there are five notations numbered 1 through 5 shown in Column I. Each notation is made up of a supplier's name, a contract number, and a date and is to be filed according to the following rules:

First: File in alphabetical order
Second: When two or more notations have the same supplier, file according to the contract number in numerical order beginning with the lowest number
Third: When two or more notations have the same supplier and contract number, file according to the date beginning with the earliest date

In Column II, the numbers 1 through 5 are arranged in four ways to show different possible orders in which the merchandise information might be filed. Pick the answer (A, B, C, or D) in Column II in which the notations are arranged according to the above filing rules.

SAMPLE QUESTION:

Column I
1. Cluney (4865) 6/17/72
2. Roster (2466) 5/10/71
3. Altool (7114) 10/15/72
4. Cluney (5276) 12/18/71
5. Cluney (4865) 4/8/72

Column II
A. 2, 3, 4, 1, 5
B. 2, 5, 1, 3, 4
C. 3, 2, 1, 4, 5
D. 3, 5, 1, 4, 2

The correct way to file the notations is:
(3) Altool (7114) 10/15/72
(5) Cluney (4865) 4/8/72
(1) Cluney (4865) 6/17/72
(4) Cluney (5276) 12/18/71
(2) Roster (2466) 5/10/71

Since the correct filing order is 3, 5, 1, 4, 2, the answer to the sample question is D.

	Column I		Column II	

1.
   1. Fenten (38511) 1/4/73
   2. Meadowlane (5020) 11/1/72
   3. Whitehall (36142) 6/22/72
   4. Clinton (4141) 5/26/71
   5. Mester (8006) 4/20/71

   A. 3, 5, 2, 1, 4
   B. 4, 1, 2, 5, 3
   C. 4, 2, 5, 3, 1
   D. 5, 4, 3, 1, 2

   1.___

2.
   1. Harvard (2286) 2/19/70
   2. Parker (1781) 4/12/72
   3. Lenson (9044) 6/6/72
   4. Brothers (38380) 10/11/72
   5. Parker (41400) 12/20/70

   A. 2, 4, 3, 1, 5
   B. 2, 1, 3, 4, 5
   C. 4, 1, 3, 2, 5
   D. 5, 2, 3, 1, 4

   2.___

3.
   1. Newtone (3197) 8/22/70
   2. Merritt (4071) 8/8/72
   3. Writebest (60666) 4/7/71
   4. Maltons (34380) 3/30/72
   5. Merrit (4071) 7/16/71

   A. 1, 4, 2, 5, 3
   B. 4, 2, 1, 5, 3
   C. 4, 5, 2, 1, 3
   D. 5, 2, 4, 3, 1

   3.___

4.
   1. Weinburt (45514) 6/4/71
   2. Owntye (35860) 10/4/72
   3. Weinburt (45515) 2/1/72
   4. Fasttex (7677) 11/10/71
   5. Owntye (4574) 7/17/72

   A. 4, 5, 2, 1, 3
   B. 4, 2, 5, 3, 1
   C. 4, 2, 5, 1, 3
   D. 4, 5, 2, 3, 1

   4.___

5.
   1. Premier (1003) 7/29/70
   2. Phylson (0031) 5/5/72
   3. Lathen (3328) 10/3/71
   4. Harper (8046) 8/18/72
   5. Lathen (3328) 12/1/72

   A. 2, 1, 4, 3, 5
   B. 3, 5, 4, 1, 2
   C. 4, 1, 2, 3, 5
   D. 4, 3, 5, 2, 1

   5.___

6.
   1. Repper (46071) 10/14/72
   2. Destex (77271) 8/27/72
   3. Clawson (30736) 7/28/71
   4. Destex (27207) 8/17/71
   5. Destex (77271) 4/14/71

   A. 3, 2, 4, 5, 1
   B. 3, 4, 2, 5, 1
   C. 3, 4, 5, 2, 1
   D. 3, 5, 4, 2, 1

   6.___

7. Assume that a clerk is asked to prepare a special report which he has not prepared before. He decides to make a written outline of the report before writing it in full. This decision by the clerk is

   A. *good,* mainly because it helps the writer to organize his thoughts and decide what will go into the report
   B. *good,* mainly because it clearly shows the number of topics, number of pages, and the length of the report
   C. *poor,* mainly because it wastes the time of the writer since he will have to write the full report anyway
   D. *poor,* mainly because it confines the writer to those areas listed in the outline

   7.___

8. Assume that a clerk in the water resources central shop is asked to prepare an important report, giving the location and condition of various fire hydrants in the city. One of the hydrants in question is broken and is spewing rusty water in the street, creating a flooded condition in the area. The clerk reports that the hydrant is broken but does not report the escaping water or the flood.
Of the following, the BEST evaluation of the clerk's decision about what to report is that it is basically

   A. *correct,* chiefly because a lengthy report would contain irrelevant information
   B. *correct,* chiefly because a more detailed description of a hydrant should be made by a fireman, not a clerk
   C. *incorrect,* chiefly because the clerk's assignment was to describe the condition of the hydrant and he should give a full explanation
   D. *incorrect,* chiefly because the clerk should include as much information as possible in his report whether or not it is relevant

8._____

Questions 9-14.

DIRECTIONS: Questions 9 through 14 are to be answered ONLY on the information contained in the following chart, which shows the number of requisitions filled by Storeroom A during each month of the year.

NUMBER OF REQUISITIONS HANDLED EACH MONTH
DURING THE YEAR BY STOREROOM A

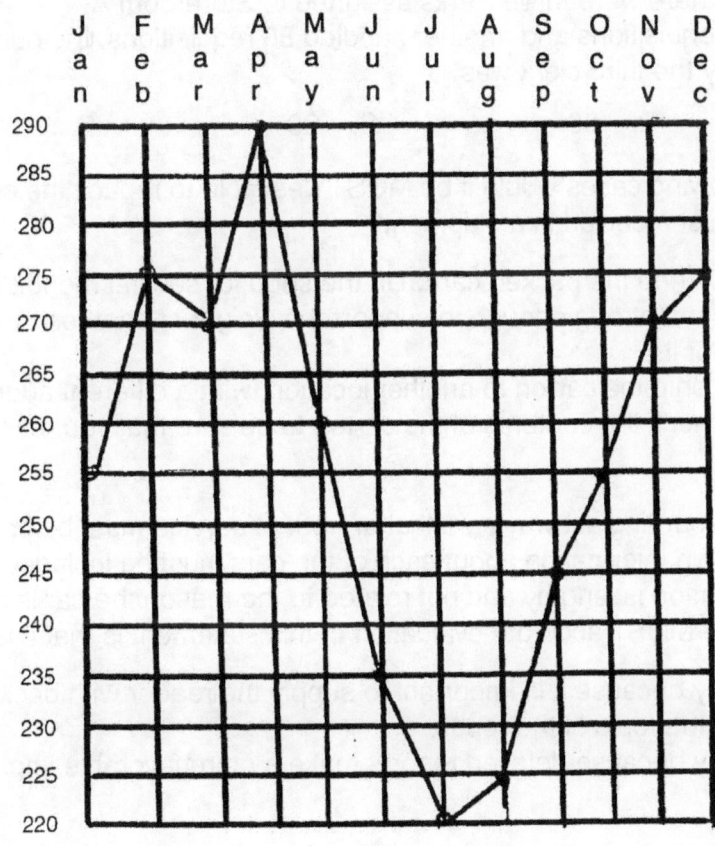

9. According to the above chart, the average number of requisitions handled per month by Storeroom A during the first six months of the year is MOST NEARLY

   A. 250 B. 260 C. 270 D. 280

10. It is expected that the number of requisitions Storeroom A will handle next year will be 10 percent more than it handled this year.
   The number of requisitions Storeroom A is expected to handle next year will MOST likely be

   A. 2,763 B. 3,070 C. 3,382 D. 3,440

11. The month during which the number of requisitions handled showed the GREATEST decrease from the previous month was

   A. April B. May C. June D. July

12. During May there were 3 clerks assigned to Storeroom A. One man went on vacation for the month of June and was not replaced.
   The number of additional orders handled by each man working in June over the number of orders handled per man in May was MOST NEARLY

   A. 20 B. 27 C. 32 D. 36

13. During June, July, and August, 8 percent of the requisitions handled were rush orders. The number of rush orders handled during these three months is MOST NEARLY

   A. 55 B. 60 C. 65 D. 70

14. During November, there were three clerks assigned to Storeroom A.
   If one handled 95 requisitions and another handled 85 requisitions, the number of requisitions handled by the third clerk was

   A. 70 B. 80 C. 90 D. 100

15. In which of the following cases would it be MOST desirable to repack the contents of a carton which was just received in a shipment?

   A. You expect to keep the packed carton in the shop for several months.
   B. The carton is not strong enough to support the weight of another carton you want to put on top of it.
   C. You intend to ship the carton to another location, with a different address.
   D. You want to check the contents of the carton to be sure that you received the correct shipment.

16. The daily reports regarding subway cars that are out of service must be prepared in great detail. All known information about each of the cars must be included in the report, even if such information is lengthy and not related to the reason the car is out of service.
   Of the following, the MOST accurate evaluation of this statement is that it is basically

   A. *correct*, mainly because it is important to supply the reader with background information about the topic of the report
   B. *correct*, mainly because detailed reports make a more favorable impression upon the reader

C. *incorrect,* mainly because a good report should be as brief as possible and contain only relevant information
D. *incorrect,* mainly because background information about each car should be supplied in a separate report

Questions 17-22.

DIRECTIONS: Questions 17 through 22 are to be answered ONLY on the basis of the information in the chart below.

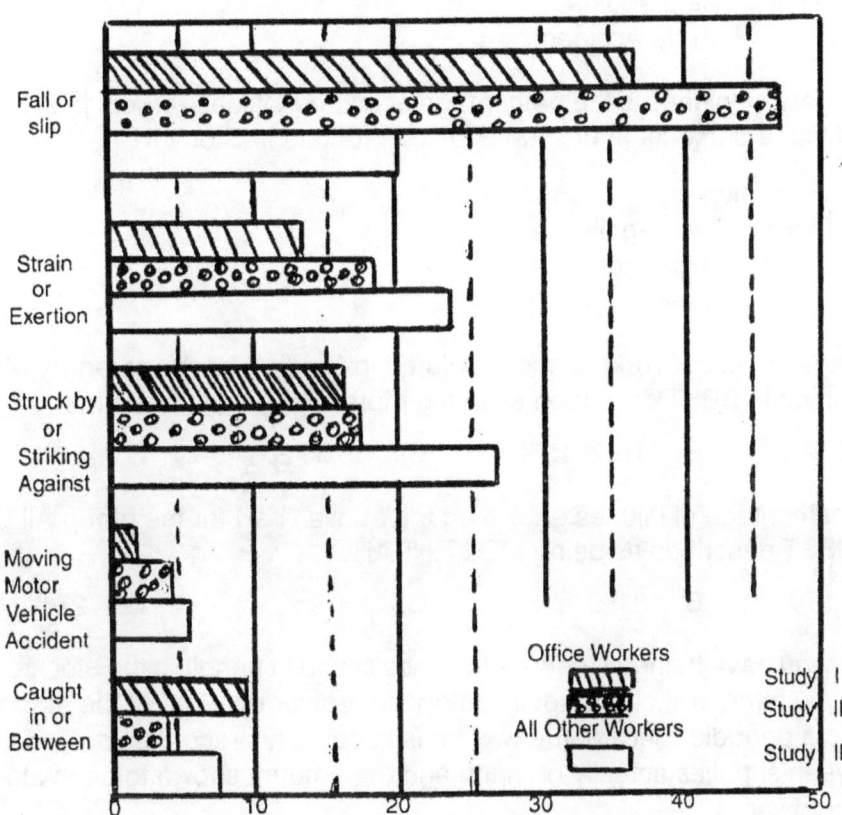

The above chart shows the results of two studies concerning injuries to office workers. Study I was done only for office workers. The results are represented by ▨, Study II compared injuries to office workers with injuries to all other workers. In Study II, office workers are represented by ▨ ; all other workers by ▢

17. In Study II, in which category of accident was there a 5% difference between the percentage of Office Workers injured and the percentage of All Other Workers injured?   17.____

    A. Strain or Exertion
    B. Struck by or Striking Against
    C. Moving Motor Vehicle Accident
    D. Caught In or Between

18. In which category of accident is the average percentage of all Office Workers injured closest to the percentage of injuries for All Other Workers? 18.___

   A. Fall or Slip
   B. Strain or Exertion
   C. Struck By or Striking Against
   D. Caught In or Between

19. In which category is the percentage of All Other Workers injured MOST NEARLY one-half of the average percentage for all Office Workers injured? 19.___

   A. Fall or Slip
   B. Strain or Exertion
   C. Struck By or Striking Against
   D. Moving Motor Vehicle Accident

20. In which category of injuries is the percentage of injured Office Workers in Study I shown to be closest to the percentage of injured Office Workers in Study II? 20.___

   A. Strain or Exertion
   B. Struck By or Striking Against
   C. Moving Motor Vehicle Accident
   D. Caught In or Between

21. The percentage of Office Workers shown injured in Study II for the category of accident Strain or Exertion is BEST described as being more than _____ less than _____ . 21.___

   A. 5%; 10%   B. 10%; 15%   C. 15%; 20%   D. 20%; 24%

22. The largest percentage of injuries shown on the above chart for the group All Other Workers is BEST described as being MOST NEARLY 22.___

   A. 18%   B. 21%   C. 24%   D. 27%

23. Suppose that you have trained a new clerk to assist you in handling the stockroom. A few weeks later, you put him in charge of inventory control for one-half of the stockroom. When making a periodic check of the way he is keeping his records, you find quite a difference between supplies actually on hand and the amount shown to be in stock on the inventory record cards. 23.___
   Of the following, the BEST action to take in this situation is to

   A. report the clerk to your supervisor because he is not keeping the records properly
   B. tell the clerk that you will order an additional supply of the items to cover the difference
   C. review the inventory control procedure with the clerk in order to locate the source of the error
   D. advise the clerk that he is not suited for this job and that you will recommend that he be transferred

24. You are the clerk in charge of the time cards on which the men in the shop sign in in the mornings and sign out in the afternoons. Suppose that one day a co-worker with whom you are especially friendly asks you to let him sign 15 minutes before the others so that he can get a seat on the subway. 24.___
   Of the following, which is the MOST desirable action to take?

A. Go on and let your friend sign out; no one will know about it except the two of you
B. Tell your friend you'll let him sign out this first time, but warn him not to ask again
C. Tell your friend you are going to report him to your supervisor and to his, so he will not try anything like this again
D. Explain to your friend that this is a violation of the rules and that, even though you're friends, you cannot grant his request

25. Suppose that one of the road crew working in a shop receives a great many personal phone calls and constantly requests the clerk to take detailed messages for him. Taking these messages is beginning to take up a lot of the clerk's time.
The BEST thing for the clerk to do under the circumstances is to

    A. tell the man's supervisor that he should put a stop to his men receiving so many personal phone calls
    B. purposely omit or confuse some messages so the worker will stop requesting that he take them
    C. explain to the worker that he cannot spend so much time taking messages because it is interfering with his work
    D. continue to take the messages, but write a report to the worker's supervisor complaining about the phone calls

26. For a six-month period including the previous months, 6 additional mechanics are assigned to work in a shop for a special assignment. The clerk must prepare a vacation schedule for all the men in the shop based on the men's requests and their seniority in the department. Several of the 12 *regulars* in the shop believe they should be given priority, and ask the clerk to do so, even though some of the other men have greater seniority.
Under the circumstances, the clerk should

    A. immediately report the *regulars* to their supervisor for trying to break the rules
    B. tell them that, since all the men are assigned to the shop, he must make up the schedule as if they were all *regulars*
    C. try to satisfy the *regulars* since they will be around as co-workers after the other 6 men leave
    D. tell the new men that some of the *regulars* are trying to make trouble for them

27. Assume that you receive a written complaint from an irate vendor shortly after your supervisor has begun his vacation. The supervisor is not expected back for several weeks. The complaint is complex, and you are uncertain about how to reply to it.
Of the following, the BEST course of action for you to take in this situation is to

    A. answer the vendor's complaint as well as you can
    B. assign a clerk in your shop to reply to the vendor's complaint
    C. wait until your supervisor returns from vacation
    D. write to the vendor to tell him that the complaint has been received and that your office is looking into it

28. Suppose that you are a clerk in a transit authority repair shop. A member of the public has called the transit authority to complain about poor ventilation in a subway car, and the call has been transferred to your office. The man demands to speak to the foreman, who is gone for the day to attend a meeting. The man becomes increasingly angry and abusive when you tell him the foreman has gone.
Under the circumstances, the BEST thing for you to do is to

A. tell the man that if he continues to yell at you you will hang up
B. try to calm the man down and then tell him you will record his complaint and report it to the foreman
C. speak to the man as loudly and rudely as he is speaking to you until he calms down
D. hang up the telephone since the man is not rational and there is no point in talking to him

29. You and a co-worker are both asked by your supervisor to work on a job that requires two men working full-time to complete it on time. You find that your co-worker is *goofing off* and not doing his share of the work.
Of the following, the FIRST thing you should do is to

A. try to do enough work for two of you, so the job will be finished on time
B. begin to goof off also, so your co-worker will not think he can take advantage of you
C. tell your co-worker that you think he is not doing his share, and that you will have to go to the supervisor if he doesn't straighten out
D. report your co-worker to your supervisor, and tell the supervisor you refuse to continue unless he assigns someone else to work with you

Questions 30-33.

DIRECTIONS: Questions 30 through 33 are to be answered on the basis of the information in the report below.

To: Chief, Division X
From: Mrs. Helen Jones, Clerk
Subject: Accident Involving Two Employees, Mr. John Smith and Mr. Robert Brown

On February 15, Mr. Smith and Mr. Brown were both injured in an accident occurring in the shop at 10 Long Road. No one was in the area of the accident other than Mr. Smith and Mr. Brown. Both of these employees described the following circumstances:

1. Mr. Brown saw the largest tool on the wall begin to fall from where it was hanging and ran up to push Mr. Smith out of the way and to prevent the tool from falling, if possible.
2. Mr. Smith was standing near the wall under some tools which were hanging on nails in the wall.
3. Mr. Brown was standing a few steps from the wall.
4. Mr. Brown stepped toward Mr. Smith, who was on the floor and away from the falling tool. He tripped and fell over a piece of equipment on the floor.
5. Mr. Brown pushed Mr. Smith who slipped on some grease on the floor and fell to the side, out of the way of the falling tool.
6. Mr. Brown tried to avoid Mr. Smith as he fell. In so doing, he fell against some pipes which were leaning against the wall. The pipes fell on both Mr. Brown and Mr. Smith.

Mr. Smith and Mr. Brown were both badly bruised and shaken. They were sent to the General Hospital to determine if any bones were broken. The office was later notified that neither employee was seriously hurt.

Since the accident, matters relating to safety and accident prevention around the shop have occupied the staff. There have been a number of complaints about the location of tools and equipment. Several employees are reluctant to work in the shop unless conditions are improved. Please advise as to the best way to handle this situation.

30. The one of the following which it is MOST important to add to the above memorandum is

    A. a signature line
    B. a transmittal note
    C. the date of the memo
    D. the initials of the typist

31. The MOST logical order in which to list the circumstances relative to the accident is

    A. as shown (1, 2, 3, 4, 5, 6)
    B. 2, 3, 1, 5, 4, 6
    C. 1, 5, 4, 6, 3, 2
    D. 3, 2, 4, 6, 1, 5

32. The one of the following which does NOT properly belong with the rest of the memorandum is

    A. the first section of paragraph 1
    B. the list of circumstances
    C. paragraph 2
    D. paragraph 3

33. According to the information in the memorandum, the BEST description of the subject is

    A. effect of accident on work output of the division
    B. description of accident involving Mr. Smith and Mr. Brown
    C. recommendations on how to avoid future accidents
    D. safety and accident control in the shop

34. The items of stock which should usually be issued FIRST are those which

    A. are of best quality
    B. are of poorest quality
    C. have been longest in the storeroom
    D. are not being stored any more

35. If all the new stock of a certain item will not fit on the shelf where the old stock is stored, it would usually be BEST to

    A. store some of the stock in a new location
    B. store the excess stock in the aisle near the shelf
    C. keep the new stock in the receiving area until the old stock is issued
    D. move all the stock to a new location

36. The MAJOR purpose of maintaining an adequate inventory is to

    A. prevent supply shortages
    B. reduce waste of storage space
    C. increase the dollar value of the organization
    D. provide enough jobs for stockmen

37. The term *This Side Up* is MOST appropriate on a carton containing

    A. canned food
    B. boxes of paper clips
    C. clothing
    D. a typewriter

38. Storeroom records are essential in order to have a supply of each stock item always available.
    What information is it NOT necessary to include in storeroom records?

    A. When to reorder stock items
    B. Required delivery time
    C. Means of transportation of delivery
    D. Sources of stock supply

39. Assume that you usually order a new supply of tires for your agency's fleet of trucks every 6 months. Just before you place an order, you find out that there is a 10% increase expected in the price of tires during the next 3 months.
    Of the following, the BEST action for you to take FIRST is to

    A. automatically order a double supply of tires before the prices are increased in order to save the 10%
    B. ignore the expected price increase because it is only expected, not definite
    C. determine what the storage and other costs for an extra order of tires will be and compare it with the cost of a 10% price increase
    D. wait until the new prices go into effect because the more expensive tires will probably be better quality

40. Assume that your supervisor asks you to do a certain job of unpacking cartons. He tells you how to do it, but you believe there is a better, faster way.
    The MOST advisable course of action for you to take is to

    A. follow your supervisor's orders and unpack the cartons his way, without comment
    B. unpack the cartons your way and then show your supervisor the result
    C. ask your co-workers which way they think is better, and do the job that way
    D. explain your way to your supervisor and then ask him which method you should use

KEY (CORRECT ANSWERS)

1. B	11. B	21. C	31. B
2. C	12. C	22. D	32. D
3. C	13. A	23. C	33. B
4. A	14. C	24. D	34. C
5. D	15. B	25. C	35. A
6. C	16. C	26. B	36. A
7. A	17. A	27. D	37. D
8. C	18. D	28. B	38. C
9. B	19. A	29. C	39. C
10. C	20. B	30. C	40. D

EXAMINATION SECTION
TEST 1

DIRECTIONS: Each question or incomplete statement is followed by several suggested answers or completions. Select the one that BEST answers the question or completes the statement. *PRINT THE LETTER OF THE CORRECT ANSWER IN THE SPACE AT THE RIGHT.*

1. The process of determining the quantity of goods and materials that are in stock is commonly called

    A. receiving
    B. disbursement
    C. reconciliation
    D. inventory

    1._____

2. Proper and effective storage procedure involves the storing of

    A. items together on the basis of class grouping
    B. all items in chronological order based on date received
    C. items in alphabetical order based on date of delivery
    D. items randomly wherever space is available

    2._____

3. Which of the following is the FIRST step involved in correctly taking an inventory?

    A. Reconciliation of inventory records with the number of items on hand
    B. Analysis of possible discrepancies between items on hand and the stock record balance
    C. Identification and recording of the locations of all items in stock
    D. Issuance of an inventory directive to all vendors

    3._____

4. Supply items other than food which are subject to deterioration should be checked

    A. at delivery time only
    B. occasionally
    C. only when issued
    D. periodically

    4._____

5. For which of the following supplies is it MOST necessary to provide ample ventilation?

    A. Small rubber parts
    B. Metal products
    C. Flammable liquids
    D. Wooden items

    5._____

6. Storing small lots of supplies in an area designated for the storage of large lots of supplies will generally result in

    A. *loss* of supplies
    B. *loss* of storage space
    C. *increase* in inventory
    D. *increase* in storage space

    6._____

7. Compliance with fire preventive measures is a major requirement for the maintenance of a safe warehouse. Which of the following statements is LEAST important in describing a measure useful in maintaining a fire preventive facility?

    A. Smoking is only permitted in designated areas.
    B. Oil-soaked rags should be disposed of promptly and not stored.
    C. When not in use, electrical machinery should be grounded.
    D. Gasoline-powered materials handling equipment should not be refueled with the motor running.

    7._____

8. It is POOR storage practice to store small valuable items loosely in open containers in bulk storage areas because doing so results in the

   A. misplacement of such items
   B. pilferage of these items
   C. deterioration of such supplies
   D. hindrance in inspection of these supplies

9. Assume that you have been placed in charge of the receiving operations at your garage. Generally, you receive all the supplies you order during the first week of each month. Of the following, the MOST effective and economic way to facilitate receiving operations would be to

   A. secure overtime authorization for laborers during that week
   B. have all truck deliveries made in one day
   C. stagger truck deliveries throughout each morning of the week
   D. assign all personnel to receiving duty for that week

10. Effective security measures must be instituted to provide for the safekeeping of city supplies.
    However, the scope and complexity of security measures used at a warehouse facility should correspond MOST NEARLY to the

    A. value of supplies stored in the warehouse
    B. borough in which the warehouse is located
    C. level of warehouse activity
    D. age of the warehouse facility

11. To facilitate handling and issuance of supply items that have a high turnover rate, they should generally be stored

    A. away from accessible aisles
    B. on upper shelves
    C. in a locked compartment area
    D. close to the service counter area

12. The MOST important factor to be considered in effectively storing heavy, bulky, and difficult-to-handle items is to store these items

    A. as close to shipping areas as possible
    B. in storage areas with a low floor-load capacity
    C. only in outside storage sheds
    D. away from aisles

Questions 13-16.

DIRECTIONS: Questions 13 through 16 are to be answered using ONLY the information in the following passage.

Fire exit drills should be established and held periodically to effectively train personnel to leave their working area promptly upon proper signal and to evacuate the building speedily but without confusion. All fire exit drills should be carefully planned and carried out in a serious manner under rigid discipline so as to provide positive protection in the event of a real emergency. As a general rule, the local fire department should be furnished advance information regarding the exact date and time the exit drill is scheduled. When it is impossible to hold regular drills, written instructions should be distributed to all employees.

Depending upon individual circumstances, fires in warehouses vary from those of fast development that are almost instantly beyond any possibility of employee control to others of relatively slow development where a small readily attackable flame may be present for periods of time up to 15 minutes or more during which simple attack with fire extinguishers or small building hoses may prevent the fire development. In any case, it is characteristic of many warehouse fires that at a certain point in development they flash up to the top of the stack, increase heat quickly, and spread rapidly. There is a degree of inherent danger in attacking warehouse type fires and all employees should be thoroughly trained in the use of the types of extinguishers or small hoses in the buildings and well instructed in the necessity of always staying between the fire and a direct pass to an exit.

13. Employees should be instructed that, when fighting a fire, they MUST

    A. try to control the blaze
    B. extinguish any fire in 15 minutes
    C. remain between the fire and a direct passage to the exit
    D. keep the fire between themselves and the fire exit

14. Whenever conditions are such that regular fire drills cannot be held, then which one of the following actions should be taken?

    A. The local fire department should be notified.
    B. Rigid discipline should be maintained during work hours.
    C. Personnel should be instructed to leave their working area by whatever means are available.
    D. Employees should receive fire drill procedures in writing.

15. The passage indicates that the purpose of fire exit drills is to train employees to

    A. control a fire before it becomes uncontrollable
    B. act as firefighters
    C. leave the working area promptly
    D. be serious

16. According to the passage, fire exit drills will prove to be of *utmost* effectiveness if

    A. employee participation is made voluntary
    B. they take place periodically
    C. the fire department actively participates
    D. they are held without advance planning

Questions 17-20.

DIRECTIONS: Questions 17 through 20 are to be answered using ONLY the information in the following paragraph.

A report is frequently ineffective because the person writing it is not fully acquainted with all the necessary details before he actually starts to construct the report. All details pertaining to the subject should be known before the report is started. If the essential facts are not known, they should be investigated. It is wise to have essential facts written down rather than to depend too much on memory, especially if the facts pertain to such matters as amounts, dates, names of persons, or other specific data. When the necessary information has been gathered, the general plan and content of the report should be thought out before the writing is actually begun. A person with little or no experience in writing reports may find that it is wise to make a brief outline. Persons with more experience should not need a written outline, but they should make mental notes of the steps they are to follow. If writing reports without dictation is a regular part of an office worker's duties, he should set aside a certain time during the day when he is least likely to be interrupted. That may be difficult, but in most offices there are certain times in the day when the callers, telephone calls, and other interruptions are not numerous. During those times, it is best to write reports that need undivided concentration. Reports that are written amid a series of interruptions may be poorly done.

17. Before starting to write an effective report, it is necessary to

    A. memorize all specific information
    B. disregard ambiguous data
    C. know all pertinent information
    D. develop a general plan

18. Reports dealing with complex and difficult material should be

    A. prepared and written by the supervisor of the unit
    B. written when there is the least chance of interruption
    C. prepared and written as part of regular office routine
    D. outlined and then dictated

19. According to the passage, employees with no prior familiarity in writing reports may find it helpful to

    A. prepare a brief outline
    B. mentally prepare a synopsis of the report's content
    C. have a fellow employee help in writing the report
    D. consult previous reports

20. In writing a report, needed information which is unclear should be

    A. disregarded   B. investigated
    C. memorized   D. gathered

KEY (CORRECT ANSWERS)

1. D
2. A
3. C
4. D
5. C

6. B
7. C
8. B
9. C
10. A

11. D
12. A
13. C
14. D
15. C

16. B
17. C
18. B
19. A
20. B

TEST 2

DIRECTIONS: Each question or incomplete statement is followed by several suggested answers or completions. Select the one that BEST answers the question or completes the statement. *PRINT THE LETTER OF THE CORRECT ANSWER IN THE SPACE AT THE RIGHT.*

Questions 1-4.

DIRECTIONS: Questions 1 through 4 are to be answered using ONLY the information in the following passage.

The operation and maintenance of the stock-location system is a warehousing function and responsibility. The stock locator system shall consist of a file of stock-location record cards, either manually or mechanically prepared, depending upon the equipment available. The file shall contain an individual card for each stock item stored in the depot, with the records maintained in stock number sequence.

The locator file is used for all receiving, warehousing, inventory, and shipping activities in the depot. The locator file must contain complete and accurate data to provide ready support to the various depot functions and activities, i.e., processing shipping documents, updating records on mechanized equipment, where applicable, supplying accurate locator information for stock selection and proper storage of receipts, consolidating storage locations of identical items not subject to shelf-life control, and preventing the consolidation of stock of limited shelf-life items. The file is also essential in accomplishing location surveys and the inventory program.

Storage of bulk stock items by "spot-location" method is generally recognized as the best means of obtaining maximum warehouse space utilization. Despite the fact that the spot location method of storage enables full utilization of storage capacity, this method may prove inefficient unless it is supplemented by adequate stock-location control, including proper layout and accurate maintenance of stock locator cards.

1. The manner in which the stock-location record cards should be filed is   1._____

    A. alphabetically   B. chronologically
    C. numerically   D. randomly

2. Items of limited shelf-life should   2._____

    A. not be stored
    B. not be stored together
    C. be stored in stock sequence
    D. be stored together

3. Which one of the following is NOT mentioned in the passage as a use of the stock-location system?   3._____
Aids in

    A. accomplishing location surveys
    B. providing information for stock selection
    C. storing items received for the first time
    D. processing shipping documents

4. If the spot-location method of storing is used, then the use of the stock-location system is　　4.____
   A. *desirable*, because the stock-location system is recognized as the best means of obtaining maximum warehouse space utilization
   B. *undesirable*, because additional records must be kept
   C. *desirable*, because stock-location controls are necessary with the spot-location storage method
   D. *undesirable*, because a stock-locator system will take up valuable storage space

Questions 5-8.

DIRECTIONS:　Questions 5 through 8 are to be answered using ONLY the information in the following paragraph.

Known damage is defined as damage that is apparent and acknowledged by the carrier at the time of delivery to the purchaser. A meticulous inspection of the damaged goods should be completed by the purchaser and a notation specifying the extent of the damage should be applied to the carrier's original freight bill. As is the case in known loss, it is necessary for the carrier's agent to acknowledge by signature the damage notation in order for it to have any legal status. The purchaser should not refuse damaged freight since it is his legal duty to accept the property and to employ every available and reasonable means to protect the shipment and minimize the loss. Acceptance of a damaged shipment does not endanger any legitimate claim the purchaser may have against the carrier for damage. If the purchaser fails to observe the legal duty to accept damaged freight, the carrier may consider it abandoned. After properly notifying the vendor and purchaser of his intentions, the carrier may dispose of the material at public sale.

5. Before disposing of an abandoned shipment, the carrier must　　5.____
   A. notify the vendor and the carrier's agent
   B. advise the vendor and purchaser of his plans
   C. notify the purchaser and the carrier's agent
   D. obtain the signature of the carrier's agent on the freight bill

6. In the case of damaged freight, the original freight bill will only have legal value if it is signed by the　　6.____
   A. carrier's agent　　　　　　　　B. purchaser
   C. vendor　　　　　　　　　　　　D. purchaser and vendor

7. A purchaser does not protect a shipment of cargo that is damaged and is further deteriorating.　　7.____
   According to the above paragraph, the action of the purchaser is
   A. *acceptable*, because he is not obligated to protect damaged cargo
   B. *unacceptable*, because damaged cargo must be protected no matter what is involved
   C. *acceptable*, because he took possession of the cargo
   D. *unacceptable*, because he is obligated by law to protect the cargo

8. The TWO requirements that must be satisfied before cargo can be labeled *known damage* are signs of evident damage and

   A. confirmation by the carrier or carrier's agent that this is so
   B. delayed shipment of goods
   C. signature of acceptance by the purchaser
   D. acknowledgment by the vendor that this is so

Questions 9-13.

DIRECTIONS: Questions 9 through 13 are to be answered on the basis of the following graph.

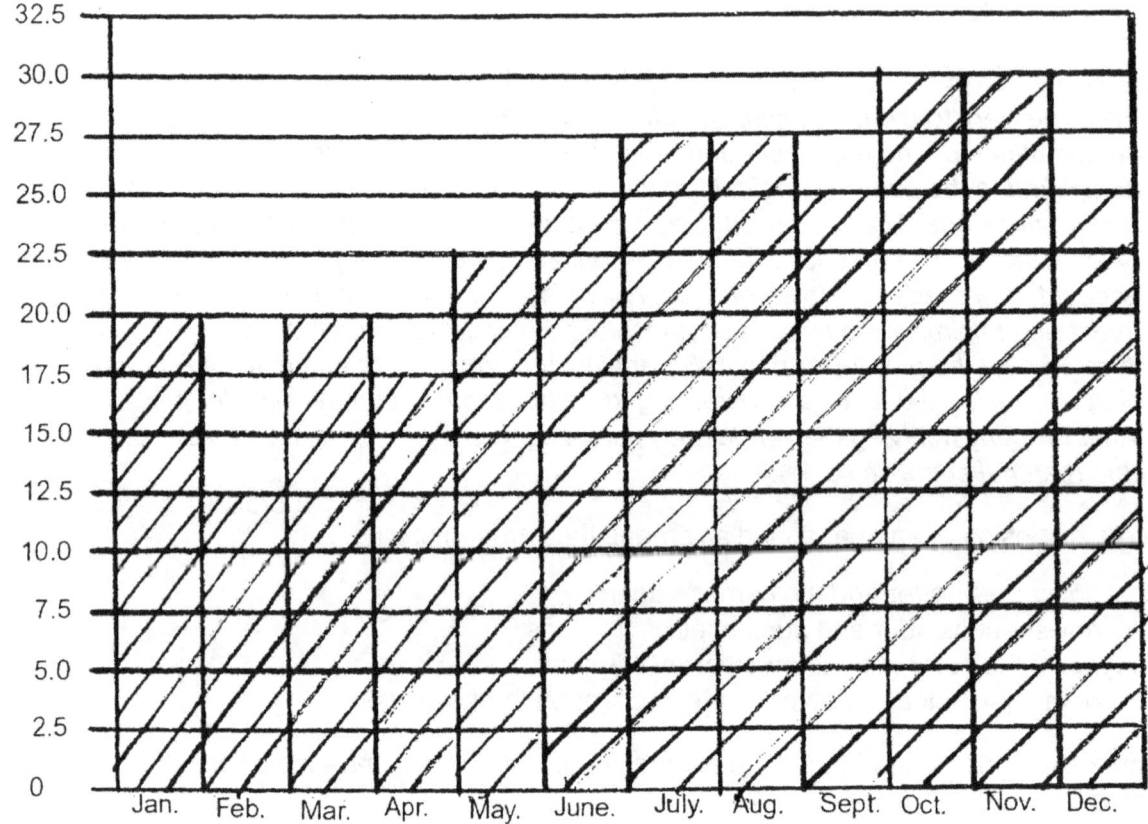

GARBAGE COLLECTIONS MADE JAN. 1 - DEC. 31, IN TONS (SHORT TON)

9. According to the information presented in the graph, the weight of the average monthly collection of garbage is MOST NEARLY _____ tons.

   A. 22.5   B. 23.5   C. 24.5   D. 25.5

10. If a truck can carry 6,000 lbs., then the number of truck-loads collected during the year was MOST NEARLY

    A. 55   B. 75   C. 95   D. 115

11. The amount of garbage collected during the second half of the year represents APPROXIMATELY what percentage of the total garbage collected during the year?

    A. 50%   B. 60%   C. 70%   D. 80%

12. During the months of September, October, and November, approximately 12% of the collections consisted of fallen leaves.
    What was the weight of the remaining garbage NOT containing fallen leaves for that period?
    _____ tons.

    A. 10   B. 20   C. 65   D. 75

13. Assume that the collections for the year as shown in the above graph exceeded the previous year's collection by 17%. The collection made in the previous year was MOST NEARLY _____ tons.

    A. 50   B. 225   C. 240   D. 275

Questions 14-17.

DIRECTIONS: Questions 14 through 17 are to be answered on the basis of the following graph

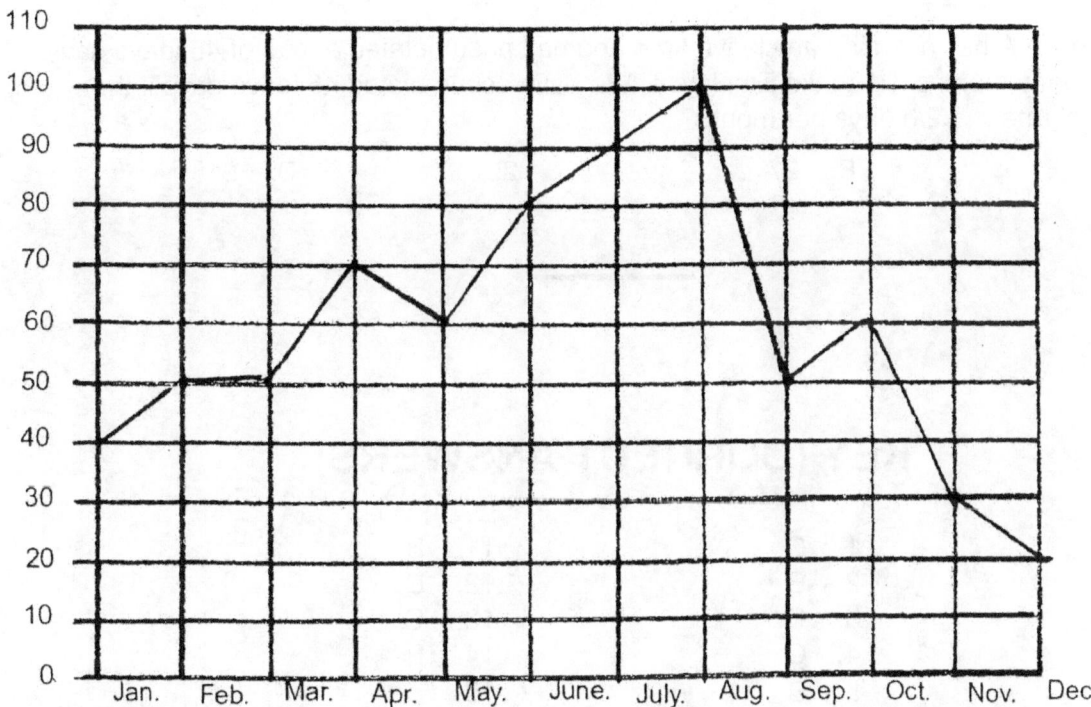

INVENTORY LEVELS (IN DOZENS) OF ITEM A IN STOREHOUSE AT BEGINNING OF MONTH FOR A PERIOD OF TWELVS MONTH

14. The average monthly inventory level during the course of the year was MOST NEARLY _____ dozen.

    A. 45   B. 60   C. 75   D. 90

15. If one dozen items fit in a carton measuring 2 feet by 2 feet by 3 feet, what MINIMUM volume would be required to store the maximum August inventory?
    _____ cubic feet.

    A. 12   B. 100   C. 700   D. 1,200

16. Assume that deliveries are made to the storehouse on the first working day of each month. If 30% of the June inventory was consumed during the month, how many items had to be delivered to reach the July inventory level?
_____ items.

   A. 288   B. 408   C. 696   D. 1,080

17. Which three-month period contained the LOWEST average inventory level?

   A. Jan., Feb., March
   B. April, May, June
   C. July, Aug., Sept.
   D. Oct., Nov., Dec.

18. Assume that it takes approximately 1 1/2 minutes to unload a dozen identical items from a delivery truck.
At this speed, the amount of time it should take to unload a shipment of 876 items is MOST NEARLY _____ minutes.

   A. 90   B. 100   C. 110   D. 120

19. Assume that a shop clerk has received a bill of $108 for a delivery of clamps which cost $4.32 per dozen.
How many clamps should there be in this delivery?

   A. 25   B. 36   C. 300   D. 360

20. Employee A has not used any leave time and has accumulated a total of 45 leave days. How many months did it take Employee A to have accumulated 45 leave days if the accrual rate is 1 2/3 days per month?

   A. 25   B. 27   C. 29   D. 31

KEY (CORRECT ANSWERS)

1.	C	11.	B
2.	B	12.	D
3.	C	13.	C
4.	C	14.	B
5.	B	15.	D
6.	A	16.	B
7.	D	17.	D
8.	A	18.	C
9.	B	19.	C
10.	C	20.	B

EXAMINATION SECTION
TEST 1

DIRECTIONS: Each question or incomplete statement is followed by several suggested answers or completions. Select the one that BEST answers the question or completes the statement. *PRINT THE LETTER OF THE CORRECT ANSWER IN THE SPACE AT THE RIGHT.*

1. A shop clerk is notified that only 75 bolts can be supplied by Vendor A. If this represents 12.5% of the total requisition, then how many bolts were *originally* ordered?

    A. 125 B. 600 C. 700 D. 900

    1.____

2. An enclosed square-shaped storage area with sides of 16 feet each has a safe-load capacity of 250 pounds per square foot.
    The MAXIMUM evenly distributed weight that can be stored in this area is _____ lbs.

    A. 1,056 B. 4,000 C. 64,000 D. 102,400

    2.____

3. A clerical employee has completed 70 progress reports the first week, 87 the second week, and 80 the third week. Assuming a 4-week month, how many progress reports must the clerk complete in the fourth week in order to attain an average of 85 progress reports per week for the month?

    A. 93 B. 103 C. 113 D. 133

    3.____

4. On the first of the month, Shop X received a delivery of 150 gallons of lubricating oil. During the month, the following amounts of oil were used on lubricating work each week: 30 quarts, 36 quarts, 20 quarts, and 48 quarts. The amount of lubricating oil *remaining* at the end of the month was _____ gallons.

    A. 4 B. 33.5 C. 41.5 D. 116.5

    4.____

5. For working a 35-hour week, Employee A earns a gross amount of $480.90. For each hour that Employee A works over 40 hours a week, he is entitled to 1 1/2 times his hourly wage rate.
    If Employee A worked 9 hours on Monday, 8 hours on Tuesday, 9 hours 30 minutes on Wednesday, 9 hours 15 minutes on Thursday, and 9 hours 15 minutes on Friday, what should his *gross* salary be for that week?

    A. $618.30 B. $632.04 C. $652.65 D. $687.00

    5.____

6. An enclosed cube-shaped storage bay has dimensions of 12 feet by 12 feet by 12 feet. Standard procedure requires that there be at least 1 foot of space between the walls, the ceiling, and the stored items.
    What is the MAXIMUM number of cube-shaped boxes with length, width, and height of 1 foot each that can be stored on 1-foot high pallets in this bay?

    A. 1,000 B. 1,331 C. 1,452 D. 1,728

    6.____

7. Assume that two ceilings are to be painted. One ceiling measures 30 feet by 15 feet and the second 45 feet by 60 feet.
    If one quart of paint will cover 60 square feet of ceiling, *approximately* how much paint will be required to paint the two ceilings? _____ gallons.

    7.____

31

A. 6   B. 10   C. 13   D. 18

8. In last year's budget, $7,500 was spent for office supplies. Of this amount, 60% was spent for paper supplies. If the price of paper has risen 20% over last year's price, then the amount that will be spent this year on paper supplies, assuming the same quantity will be purchased, will be

    A. $3,600   B. $5,200   C. $5,400   D. $6,000

Questions 9-13.

DIRECTIONS: Questions 9 through 13 are to be answered on the basis of the following information.

A certain shop keeps an informational card file on all suppliers and merchandise. On each card is the supplier's name, the contrast number for the merchandise he supplies, and a delivery date for the merchandise. In this filing system, the supplier's name is filed alphabetically, the contract number for the merchandise is filed numerically, and the delivery date is filed chronologically.

In Questions 9 through 13, there are five notations numbered 1 through 5 shown in Column I. Each notation is made up of a supplier's name, a contract number, and a date which is to be filed according to the following rules:

    First: File in alphabetical order
    Second: When two or more notations have the same supplier, file according to the contract number in numerical order beginning with the lowest number
    Third: When two or more notations have the same supplier and contract number, file according to the date beginning with the earliest date.

In Column II, the numbers 1 through 5 are arranged in four ways to show four different orders in which the merchandise information might be filed. Pick the answer (A, B, C, or D) in Column II in which the notations are arranged according to the above filing rules.

SAMPLE QUESTION:

COLUMN I   COLUMN II

1. Cluney (4865) 6/17/05   A. 2, 3, 4, 1, 5

2. Roster (2466) 5/10/04   B. 2, 5, 1, 3, 4

3. Altool (7114) 10/15/05   C. 3, 2, 1, 4, 5

4. Cluney (5276) 12/18/04   D. 3, 5, 1, 4, 2

5. Cluney (4865) 4/8/05

The CORRECT way to file the cards is:

3. Altool (7114) 10/15/05
5. Cluney (4865) 4/8/05
1. Cluney (4865) 6/17/05
4. Cluney (5276) 12/18/04
2. Roster (2466) 5/10/04

Since the correct filing order is 3, 5, 1, 4, 2, the answer to the sample question is D.

<u>COLUMN I</u>   <u>COLUMN II</u>

9.
1. Warren (96063) 3/30/06
2. Moore (21237) 9/4/07
3. Newman (10050) 12/12/06
4. Downs (81251) 1/2/06
5. Oliver (60145) 6/30/07

A. 2, 4, 3, 5, 1
B. 2, 3, 5, 4, 1
C. 4, 5, 2, 3, 1
D. 4, 2, 3, 5, 1

9.____

10.
1. Henry (40552) 7/6/07
2. Boyd (91251) 9/1/06
3. George (8196) 12/12/06
4. George (31096) 1/12/07
5. West (6109) 8/9/06

A. 5, 4, 3, 1, 2
B. 2, 3, 4, 1, 5
C. 2, 4, 3, 1, 5
D. 5, 2, 3, 1, 4

10.____

11.
1. Salba (4670) 9/7/06
2. Salba (51219) 3/1/06
3. Crete (81562) 7/1/07
4. Salba (51219) 1/11/07
5. Texi (31549) 1/25/06

A. 5, 3, 1, 2, 4
B. 3, 1, 2, 4, 5
C. 3, 5, 4, 2, 1
D. 5, 3, 4, 2, 1

11.____

12.
1. Crayone (87105) 6/10/07
2. Shamba (49210) 1/5/06
3. Valiant (3152) 5/1/07
4. Valiant (3152) 1/9/07
5. Poro (59613) 7/1/06

A. 1, 2, 5, 3, 4
B. 1, 5, 2, 3, 4
C. 1, 5, 3, 4, 2
D. 1, 5, 2, 4, 3

12.____

13.
1. Mackie (42169) 12/20/06
2. Lebo (5198) 9/12/05
3. Drummon (99631) 9/9/07
4. Lebo (15311) 1/25/05
5. Harvin (81765) 6/2/06

A. 3, 2, 1, 5, 4
B. 3, 2, 4, 5, 1
C. 3, 5, 2, 4, 1
D. 3, 5, 4, 2, 1

13.____

Questions 14-18.

DIRECTIONS: Questions 14 through 18 are to be answered on the basis of the following information.

In order to make sure stock is properly located, incoming units are stored as follows:

<u>Stock Numbers</u>	<u>Bin Numbers</u>
00100 - 39999	D30, L44
40000 - 69999	I4L, D38
70000 - 99999	41L, 80D
100000 and over	614, 83D

Using the above table, choose the answer (A, B, C, or D) which lists the correct bin number for the stock number given.

14. 17243

    A. 41L   B. 83D   C. I4L   D. D30

15. 9219

    A. D38   B. L44   C. 614   D. 41L

16. 90125

    A. 41L   B. 614   C. D38   D. D30

17. 10001

    A. L44   B. D38   C. SOD   D. 83D

18. 200100

    A. 41L   B. I4L   C. 83D   D. D30

19. A supervisor believes that the current filing systems used in his office are not efficient. When his superior goes on vacation, he intends to change all the filing procedures.
    For a supervisor to undertake this move without his superior's knowledge would GENERALLY be considered

    A. *advisable*; it shows that he has initiative
    B. *inadvisable*; the current filing systems are probably the best
    C. *advisable*; the result will be an increase in productivity
    D. *inadvisable*; the supervisor should be informed of any intended changes

20. Assume that you have been assigned the task of handling all telephone calls at a sanitation garage. After a recent snowstorm, your supervisor informed you that all available personnel have been assigned to snow removal duties. However, you have been receiving numerous telephone calls from the public in regard to unshoveled streets and intersections.
    In handling these calls, it is generally considered good policy by the department to

    A. indicate to the callers that the department is clearing streets off as quickly as possible
    B. tell the callers there is nothing that can be done
    C. tell the callers that they are tying up departmental telephones with needless complaints
    D. promise the callers that streets will be cleared by the evening

KEY (CORRECT ANSWERS)

1. B
2. C
3. B
4. D
5. C

6. A
7. C
8. C
9. D
10. B

11. B
12. D
13. C
14. D
15. B

16. A
17. A
18. C
19. D
20. A

TEST 2

DIRECTIONS: Each question or incomplete statement is followed by several suggested answers or completions. Select the one that BEST answers the question or completes the statement. *PRINT THE LETTER OF TEE CORRECT ANSWER IN THE SPACE AT THE RIGHT.*

Questions 1-10.

DIRECTIONS: Questions 1 through 10 are to be answered on the basis of the following information.

A code number for any item is obtained by combining the date of delivery, number of units received, and number of units used.

The first two digits represent the day of the month, the third and fourth digits represent the month, and the fifth and sixth digits represent the year.

The number following the letter R represents the number of units received and the number following the letter U represents the number of units used.

For example, the code number 120673-R5690-U1001 indicates that a delivery of 5,690 units was made on June 12, of which 1,001 units were used.

Using the chart below, answer Questions 1 through 6 by choosing the letter (A, B, C, or D) in which the supplier and stock number correspond to the code number given.

Supplier	Stock Number	Number of Units Received	Delivery Date	Number of Units Used
Stony	38390	8300	May 11	3800
Stoney	39803	1780	September 15	1703
Nievo	21220	5527	October 10	5007
Nieve	38903	1733	August 5	1703
Monte	39213	5527	October 10	5007
Stony	38890	3308	December 9	3300
Stony	83930	3880	September 12	380
Nevo	47101	485	June 11	231
Nievo	12122	5725	May 11	5201
Neve	47101	9721	August 15	8207
Nievo	21120	2275	January 7	2175
Rosa	41210	3821	March 3	2710
Stony	38890	3308	September 12	3300
Dinal	54921	1711	April 2	1117
Stony	33890	8038	March 5	3300
Dinal	54721	1171	March 2	717
Claridge	81927	3308	April 5	3088
Nievo	21122	4878	June 7	3492
Haley	39670	8300	December 23	5300

1. Code No. 120972-R3308-U3300   1._____

    A. Nievo - 12122   B. Stony - 83930
    C. Nievo - 21220   D. Stony - 38890

2. Code No. 101072-R5527-U5007

    A. Nievo - 21220   B. Haley - 39670
    C. Monte - 39213   D. Claridge - 81927

3. Code No. 101073-R5527-U5007

    A. Nievo - 21220   B. Monte - 39213
    C. Nievo - 12122   D. Nievo - 21120

4. Code No. 110573-R5725-U5201

    A. Nievo - 12122   B. Nievo - 21220
    C. Haley - 39670   D. Stony - 38390

5. Code No. 070172-R2275-U2175

    A. Stony - 33890   B. Stony - 83930
    C. Stony - 38390   D. Nievo - 21120

6. Code No. 120972-R3880-U380

    A. Stony - 83930   B. Stony - 38890
    C. Stony - 33890   D. Monte - 39213

Using the same chart, answer Questions 7 through 10, choosing the letter (A, B, C, or D) in which the code number corresponds to the supplier and stock number given.

7. Nieve - 38903

    A. 951973-R1733-U1703   B. 080572-R1733-U1703
    C. 080573-R1733-U1703   D. 050873-R1733-U1703

8. Nevo - 47101

    A. 081573-R9721-U8207   B. 091573-R9721-U8207]
    C. 110672-R485-U231   D. 061172-R485-U231

9. Dinal - 54921

    A. 020473-R1711-U1117   B. 030272-R1171-U717
    C. 020372-R1171-U717   D. 421973-R1711-U1117

10. Nievo - 21122

    A. 070672-R4878-U3492   B. 060772-R4878-U349
    C. 761972-R4878-U3492   D. 060772-R4878-U3492

11. A citizen who has called the office at which you are working has started yelling on the telephone. He is annoyed because he has been switched from office to office and still has not reached the proper party.
Of the following, the BEST practice to follow is to

    A. hang up on this individual since he is obviously a troublemaker
    B. yell back at him for being so childish
    C. tell him that you have heard that complaint before
    D. try to calm this person and help him reach the proper party

12. Which of the following is the MOST likely result of employees publicly criticizing the activities of their agency?
    The

    A. employees will be terminated for the good of the agency
    B. public's respect for the agency may decrease
    C. productive members of the agency may resign
    D. agency may sue these employees for libel

13. It is essential for city employees who deal with the public to provide service as promptly and completely as possible.
    Letters from the public lodging complaints regarding poor service should GENERALLY be handled by

    A. answering them as soon as possible according to agency procedures
    B. ignoring them, since only troublemakers usually write such letters
    C. returning them, since the city government does not respond to public complaints
    D. acknowledging them with no further action necessary

14. While checking the work of a clerk who is under your supervision, you notice that he has made the same mistake a number of times.
    In order to help prevent this clerk from making the same mistake again, it would be BEST for you to take which of the following courses of action?

    A. Correct the errors yourself and not mention it to the clerk
    B. Provide training for the clerk
    C. Reprimand the clerk for the mistakes made
    D. Remind the clerk of the errors he has previously made

15. A community resident calls the sanitation garage in which you are working to inquire about the days in which old furniture can be put on the street for collection. Although your unit is responsible for these collections, you do not have this information and there is nobody in the office to assist you.
    Of the following, it would be MOST advisable to

    A. tell the citizen to call back in an hour
    B. get the citizen's telephone number and inform him that you will call back when you get the information
    C. switch the call to another unit and let them get the information
    D. put the caller on hold and try to find someone that has the answer

16. As a supervisor, you have been given the responsibility of maintaining attendance records for your garage. A co-worker, who has been late a number of times, has asked you to overlook his recent lateness since it involves only ten minutes. He has been warned previously for lateness and will receive some kind of disciplinary action because of this recent lateness, for you to overlook the lateness would be

    A. *advisable;* it involves only a matter of ten minutes
    B. *inadvisable;* this employee should have to suffer the consequences of his actions
    C. *advisable;* morale in the unit will improve
    D. *inadvisable;* employee lateness should never be excused

17. When a supervisor answers incoming telephone calls, it is important for him to FIRST

    A. identify himself and/or his office
    B. ask the caller to state the reason for the call
    C. ask the caller the nature of the call
    D. ask the caller to identify himself

18. It appears to you that the current mail distribution procedures are inefficient.
    For you to make a suggestion to your supervisor for the implementation of new procedures, would be

    A. *advisable;* if the supervisor thinks your ideas are worthwhile;they may be implemented
    B. *inadvisable;* supervisors generally are not interested in changing procedures
    C. *advisable;* new procedures generally provide better results than old procedures
    D. *inadvisable;* only methods analysts should suggest changes in procedures

19. As a supervisor, you direct the work of two clerks. Recently, you discovered that one of the two clerks generally loafs around on Friday afternoons. This past Friday, you saw this particular employee standing around conversing with several employees. At that point, you severely reprimanded this employee in the presence of the other employees.
    For you to have reprimanded this employee in such a fashion was

    A. *advisable;* this employee *had it coming*
    B. *inadvisable;* you should have spoken to him privately
    C. *advisable;* this reprimand also served as a warning to the others
    D. *inadvisable;* employees should not be reprimanded

20. As a supervisor, you have been assigned to maintain garage supplies. Recently, a co-worker requested a quantity of nails and screws for use in his home. Since this involves only a small amount of supplies, he felt it would not be wrong to make such a request.
    In this case, it would be ADVISABLE for you to

    A. give the co-worker the supplies
    B. remind the co-worker that city supplies are only for city use
    C. notify the investigation department in regard to this employee
    D. forget the incident

KEY (CORRECT ANSWERS)

1.	D	11.	D
2.	C	12.	B
3.	A	13.	A
4.	A	14.	B
5.	D	15.	B
6.	A	16.	B
7.	D	17.	A
8.	C	18.	A
9.	A	19.	B
10.	A	20.	B

EXAMINATION SECTION
TEST 1

DIRECTIONS: Each question or incomplete statement is followed by several suggested answers or completions. Select the one that BEST answers the question or completes the statement. *PRINT THE LETTER OF THE CORRECT ANSWER IN THE SPACE AT THE RIGHT.*

Questions 1-10.

DIRECTIONS: Questions 1 through 10 are to be answered on the basis of the following information.

Assume you are in charge of ordering the following supplies for Unit X:

DESCRIPTION	REORDER ONLY WHEN AMOUNT FALLS TO:	AMOUNT OF EACH REORDER
Copier paper (500 pkgs/ream)	15 reams	20 reams
Copier fluid (5 bottles/carton)	2 cartons	15 cartons
Copier toner (4 bottles/pack)	1 pack	10 packs
Writing pads (12 pads/pack)	4 packs	10 packs
Typing paper (500 pkgs/ream)	3 reams	15 reams
Correction fluid (12 bottles/carton)	1 carton	5 cartons

You should assume that no supplies are reordered more than once in any one week, and that no reordering was done the first week. Reorders occur only when stated, when the facts indicate supplies have fallen below the level required, or when the facts show logically that reordering must have occurred in order for the given totals to make sense. All reorders are filled the same day they are requested.

Other important facts:

Twenty bottles of copier fluid were used in the first week.

The amount of copier fluid at the beginning of the fourth week was double the amount of copier fluid in the unit at the beginning of the first week.

Eight bottles of copier toner were used in the first week.

Forty writing pads were used in week one, and fifty writing pads were used in week two.

2 (#1)

The unit had twice as many cartons of correction fluid at the beginning of the first week as it had at the beginning of the third week.

In the first week, twenty-seven reams of copier paper were used.

A total of six reams of copier paper were used in the second and third weeks.

There were twelve reams of typing paper in the unit at the beginning of the third week.
Now that you have the facts, here is a table to help you in answering the questions that follow. Please note that some information has already been provided. All figures in the table are in terms of reams, packs, or cartons.

	Copier paper	Copier fluid	Copier toner	Writing pads	Typing paper	Correction fluid
Beginning of week 1	42			11		
Beginning of week 2		3	2		5	
Beginning of week 3						2
Beginning of week 4						

1. How many reams of copier paper were left in the unit at the beginning of the fourth week?

    A. 9 B. 16 C. 29 D. 41

2. How many cartons of copier fluid were in the unit at the beginning of the first week?

    A. 7 B. 5 C. 23 D. 18

3. How many cartons of copier fluid were used in the unit in the second and third weeks if copier fluid was only reordered once during this time?

    A. 4
    B. 28
    C. 11
    D. Cannot be determined from the information given

4. How many packs of copier toner did the unit have at the beginning of the first week?

    A. 12 B. 4 C. 6 D. 1

5. If the unit used a total of sixteen bottles of copier toner in the second and third weeks, how many bottles did the unit have at the beginning of the fourth week? Assume that the copier fluid was only reordered once during this time.

   A. 8   B. 6   C. 24   D. 32

6. Writing pads were reordered the first time in week

   A. one   B. two   C. three   D. four

7. The number of packs of writing pads at the beginning of the fifth week was half the amount of the number of packs of writing pads left at the beginning of the third week. How many writing pads were left at the beginning of the fifth week?

   A. 6.75   B. 7   C. 81   D. 84

8. How many reams of typing paper were used by the unit in the second week?

   A. 8   B. 7   C. 12   D. 15

9. How many bottles of correction fluid did the unit use in the first and second weeks if none were reordered during this time?

   A. 2   B. 6   C. 12   D. 24

10. In the third week, fourteen bottles of correction fluid were used. This means that correction fluid was reordered

    A. the second week
    B. the third week
    C. the fourth week
    D. there was no need to reorder

KEY (CORRECT ANSWERS)

1. C
2. A
3. A
4. B
5. D

6. B
7. C
8. A
9. D
10. B

READING COMPREHENSION
UNDERSTANDING AND INTERPRETING WRITTEN MATERIAL
EXAMINATION SECTION
TEST 1

DIRECTIONS: All questions are to be answered SOLELY on the basis of the information contained in the passage. Each question or incomplete statement is followed by several suggested answers or completions. Select the one that BEST answers the question or completes the statement. *PRINT THE LETTER OF THE CORRECT ANSWER IN THE SPACE AT THE RIGHT.*

Questions 1-3.

The equipment in a mail room may include a mail-metering machine. This machine simultaneously stamps, postmarks, seals, and counts letters as fast as the operator can feed them. It can also print the proper postage directly on a gummed strip to be affixed to bulky items. It is equipped with a meter which is removed from the machine and sent to the post-master to be set for a given number of stampings of any denomination. The setting of the meter must be paid for in advance. One of the advantages of metered mail is that it bypasses the cancellation operation and, thereby, facilitates handling by the post office. Mail metering also makes the pilfering of stamps impossible, but does not prevent the passage of personal mail in company envelopes through the meters unless there is established a rigid control or censorship over outgoing mail.

1. According to this statement, the postmaster
   A. is responsible for training new clerks in the use of mail-metering machines
   B. usually recommends that both large and small firms adopt the use of mail metering machines
   C. is responsible for setting the meter to print a fixed number of stampings
   D. examines the mail-metering machines to see that they are properly installed in the mail room

   1.____

2. According to this statement, the use of mail-metering machines
   A. requires the employment of more clerks in a mail room than does the use of postage stamps
   B. interferes with the handling of large quantities of outgoing mail
   C. does not prevent employees from sending their personal letters at company expense
   D. usually involves smaller expenditures for mail room equipment than does the use of postage stamps

   2.____

3. On the basis of this statement, it is MOST accurate to state that
   A. mail-metering machines are often used for opening envelopes
   B. postage stamps are generally used when bulky packages are to be mailed
   C. the use of metered mail tends to interfere with rapid mail handling by the post office
   D. mail-metering machines can seal and count letters at the same time

   3.____

Questions 4-8.

It is the Housing Administration's policy that all tenants, whether new or transferring from one housing development to another, shall be required to pay a standard security deposit of one month's rent based on the rent at the time of admission. There are, however, certain exceptions to this policy. Employees of the Administration shall not be required to pay a security deposit if they secure an apartment in an Administration development. Where the payment of a full security deposit may present a hardship to a tenant, the development's manager may allow a tenant to move into an apartment upon payment of only part of the security deposit. In such cases, however, the tenant must agree to gradually pay the balance of the deposit. If a tenant transfers from one apartment to another within the same project, the security deposit originally paid by the tenant for his former apartment will be acceptable for his new apartment, even if the rent in the new apartment is greater than the rent in the former one. Finally, tenants who receive public assistance need not pay a security deposit before moving into an apartment if the appropriate agency states, in writing, that it will pay the deposit. However, it is the responsibility of the development's manager to make certain that payment shall be received within one month of the date the tenant moves into the apartment.

4. According to the above passage, when a tenant transfers from one apartment to another in the same development, the Housing Administration will 4.____
   A. accept the tenant's old security deposit as the security deposit for his new apartment
   B. refund the tenant's old security deposit and not require him to pay a new deposit
   C. keep the tenant's old security deposit and require him to pay a new deposit
   D. require the tenant to pay a new security deposit based on the difference between his old rent and his new rent

5. On the basis of the above passage, it is INCORREC to state that a tenant who receives public assistance may move into an Administration development if 5.____
   A. he pays the appropriate security deposit
   B. the appropriate agency gives a written indication that it will pay the security deposit before the tenant moves in
   C. the appropriate agency states, by telephone, that it will pay the security deposit
   D. the appropriate agency writes the manager to indicate that the security deposit will be paid within one month but not less than two weeks from the date the tenant moves into the apartment

6. On the basis of the above passage, a tenant who transfers from an apartment in one development to an apartment in a different department will 6.____
   A. forfeit his old security deposit and be required to pay another deposit
   B. have his old security deposit refunded and not have to pay a new deposit
   C. pay the difference between his old security deposit and the new one
   D. have to pay a security deposit based on the new apartment's rent

7. The Housing Administration will NOT require payment of a security deposit if a tenant
   A. is an Administration employee
   B. is receiving public assistance
   C. claims that payment will present a hardship
   D. indicates, in writing, that he will be responsible for any damage done to his apartment

8. Of the following, the BEST title for the above passage is:
   A. Security Deposits – Transfers
   B. Security Deposits – Policy
   C. Exemptions and Exceptions – Security Deposits
   D. Amounts – Security Deposits

Questions 9-11.

Terrazzo flooring will last a very long time if it is cared for properly. Lacquers, shellac or varnish preparations should never be used on terrazzo. Soap cleaners are not recommended, since they dull the appearance of the floor. Alkaline solutions are harmful, so neutral cleaner or non-alkaline synthetic detergents will give best results. If the floor is very dirty, it may be necessary to scrub it. The same neutral cleaning solution should be used for scrubbing as for mopping. Scouring powder may be sprinkled at particularly dirty spots. Do not use steel wool for scrubbing. Small pieces of steel filings left on the floor will rust and discolor the terrazzo. Non-woven nylon or open-mesh fabric abrasive pads are suitable for scrubbing terrazzo floors.

9. According to the above passage, the BEST cleaning agent for terrazzo flooring is a(n)
   A. soap cleaner
   B. varnish preparation
   C. neutral cleaner
   D. alkaline solution

10. According to the above passage, terrazzo floors should NOT be scrubbed with
    A. non-woven nylon abrasive pads
    B. steel wool
    C. open-mesh fabric abrasive pads
    D. scouring powder

11. As used in the above passage, the word *discolor* means MOST NEARLY
    A. crack   B. scratch   C. dissolve   D. stain

Questions 12-15.

Planning for the unloading of incoming trucks is not easy since generally little or no advance notice of truck arrivals is received. The height of the floor of truck bodies and loading platforms sometimes are different; this makes necessary the use of special unloading methods. When available, hydraulic ramps compensate for the differences in platform and truck floor levels. When hydraulic ramps are not available, forklift equipment can sometimes be used, if the truck sprigs are strong enough to support such equipment. In a situation like this, the unloading operation does not differ much from unloading a railroad box car in the cases where the forklift truck or a hydraulic pallet jack cannot be used inside the truck, a pallet dolly should be placed inside the truck, so that the empty pallet can be loaded close to the truck contents and rolled easily to the truck door and platform.

12. According to the above passage, unloading trucks are 12.____
    A. easy to plan since the time of arrival is usually known beforehand
    B. the same as loading a railroad box car
    C. hard to plan since trucks arrive without notice
    D. a very normal thing to do

13. According to the above passage, which materials-handling equipment can 13.____
    make up for the difference in platform and truck floor levels?
    A. Hydraulic jacks   B. Hydraulic ramps
    C. Forklift trucks   D. Conveyors

14. According to the above passage, what materials-handling equipment can be 14.____
    used when a truck cannot support the weight of forklift equipment?
    A. A pallet dolly   B. A hydraulic ramp
    C. Bridge plates   D. A warehouse tractor

15. Which of the following is the BEST title for the above passage? 15.____
    A. Unloading Railroad Box Cars   B. Unloading Motor Trucks
    C. Loading Rail Box   D. Loading Motor Trucks

Questions 16-19.

Ventilation, as used in firefighting operations, means opening up a building or structure in which a fire is burning to release the accumulated heat, smoke, and gases. Lack of knowledge of the principle of ventilation on the part of firemen may result in unnecessary punishment due to ventilation being neglected or improperly handled. While ventilation itself extinguishes no fires, when used in an intelligent manner, it allows firemen to get at the fire more quickly, easily, and with less danger and hardship.

16. According to the above passage, the MOST important result of failure to apply 16.____
    the principles of ventilation at a fire may be
    A. loss of public confidence   B. disciplinary action
    C. waste of water   D. excessive use of equipment
    E. injury to fireman

17. It may be inferred from the above passage that the CHIEF advantage of 17.____
    ventilation is that it
    A. eliminates the need for gas masks
    B. reduces smoke damage
    C. permits firemen to work closer to the fire
    D. cools the fire
    E. enables firemen to use shorter hose lines

18. Knowledge of the principles of ventilation, as defined in the above passage, 18.____
    would be LEAST important in a fire in a
    A. tenement house   B. grocery store   C. ship's hold
    D. lumberyard   E. office building

19. We may conclude from the above passage that, for the well-trained and equipped fireman, ventilation is
    A. a simple matter
    B. rarely necessary
    C. relatively unimportant
    D. a basic tool
    E. sometimes a handicap

19.____

Questions 20-22.

Many public service and industrial organizations are becoming increasingly insistent that supervisors at the work level be qualified instructors. The reason for this is that technological improvements and overall organizational growth require the acquisition of new skills and knowledge by workers. These skills and knowledge can be acquired in two ways. They can be gained either by absorption-rubbing shoulders with the job or through planned instruction. Permitting the acquisition of new skills and knowledge is to be haphazard and uncertain is too costly. At higher supervisory levels, the need for instructing subordinate is not so obvious, but it is just as important as at the lowest work level. A high-ranking supervisor accomplishes the requirements of his position only if his subordinate supervisors perform their work efficiently. Regardless of one's supervisory position, the ability to instruct easily and efficiently helps to insure well-qualified and thoroughly-trained subordinates. There exists an unfounded but rather prevalent belief that becoming a competent instructor is a long, arduous, and complicated process. This belief arises partially as a result of the requirement of a long period of college preparation involved in preparing teachers for our school system. This time is necessary because teachers must learn a great deal of subject matter. The worker who advances to a supervisory position generally has superior skill and knowledge; therefore, he has only to learn the techniques by which he can impart his knowledge in order to become a competent instructor.

20. According to the above passage, a prolonged period of preparation for instructing is NOT generally necessary for a worker who is advanced to a supervisory position because
    A. he may already possess some of the requirements of a competent instructor
    B. his previous job knowledge is generally sufficient to enable him to begin instructing immediately
    C. in his present position there is less need for the specific job knowledge of the ordinary worker
    D. the ability to instruct follows naturally from superior skill and knowledge

20.____

21. According to the above passage, it is important for the higher-level supervisor to be a good instructor because
    A. at this level there is a tendency to overlook the need for instruction of both subordinate supervisors and workers
    B. good training practices will then be readily adopted by lower-level supervisors
    C. the need for effective training is more critical at the higher levels of responsibility
    D. training can be used to improve the supervisory performance of his subordinate supervisors

21.____

22. According to the above passage, the acquisition of new skills and knowledge by workers is BEST accomplished when
    A. the method of training allows for the use of absorption
    B. organizational growth and technological improvement indicate a need for further training
    C. such training is the result of careful planning
    D. the cost factor involved in training can be readily justified

22.____

Questions 23-25.

The organization of any large agency falls into three broad general zones: top management, middle management, and rank-and-file operations. The normal task of middle management is to supervise, direct, and control the performance of operations within the scope of law, policy, and regulations already established. Where policy is settled and well defined, middle management is basically a set of standard operations, although they may call for high-developed skills. Where, however, policy is not clearly stated, is ambiguous, or is rapidly shifting, middle management is likely to have an important influence upon emergency policy trends. Persons working in the zone of middle management usually become specialists. They need specialist knowledge of law, rules, and regulations, and court decisions governing their organization if they are to discharge their duties effectively. They will also have acquired specialist knowledge of relationships and sequences in the normal flow of business. Further, their attention is brought to bear on a particular administrative task, in a particular jurisdiction, with a particular clientele. The importance of middle management is obviously great. The reasons for such importance are not difficult to find: Here it is that the essential action of government in behalf of citizens is taken; here it is that citizens deal with government when they pass beyond their first contacts; here is a training ground from which a considerable part of top management emerges; and here it is that the spirit and temper of the public service and its reputation are largely made.

23. According to the above passage, the critical importance of middle management is due to the fact that it is at this level that
    A. formal executive training can be most useful
    B. the greatest amount of action is taken on the complaints of the general public
    C. the official actions taken have the greatest impact on general attitudes towards the public service
    D. the public most frequently comes in contact with governmental operations and agencies

23.____

24. According to the above passage, the one of the following statements which is NOT offered as an explanation of the tendency for middle management responsibility to produce specialists is that
    A. middle-management personnel frequently feel that their work is the most important in an organization
    B. specialized knowledge is acquired during the course of everyday work
    C. specialized knowledge is necessary for effective job performance
    D. their work assignments are directed to specific problems in specific situations

24.____

25. According to the above passage, the GREATEST impact of middle management in policy determination would be likely to be felt in the situation in which
   A. middle management possesses highly developed operational skills
   B. several policy directives from top management are subject to varying interpretations
   C. the authority of middle management to supervise, direct, and control operations has been clearly established
   D. top management has neglected to consider the policy views of middle management

KEY (CORRECT ANSWERS)

1. C
2. C
3. D
4. A
5. C

6. D
7. A
8. B
9. C
10. B

11. D
12. C
13. B
14. A
15. B

16. E
17. C
18. D
19. D
20. A

21. D
22. C
23. C
24. A
25. B

TEST 2

DIRECTIONS: All questions are to be answered SOLELY on the basis of the information contained in the passage. Each question or incomplete statement is followed by several suggested answers or completions. Select the one that BEST answers the question or completes the statement. *PRINT THE LETTER OF THE CORRECT ANSWER IN THE SPACE AT THE RIGHT.*

Questions 1-2.

Metal spraying is used for many purposes. Worn bearings on shafts and spindles can be readily restored to original dimensions with any desired metal or alloy. Low-carbon steel shafts may be supplied with high-carbon steel journal surfaces, which can then be ground to size after spraying. By using babbitt wire, bearings can be lined or babbited while rotating. Pump shafts and impellers can be coated with any desired metal to overcome wear and corrosion. Valve seats may be re-surfaced. Defective castings can be repaired by filling in blowholes and checks. The application of metal spraying to the field of corrosion resistance is growing, although the major application in this field is in the use of sprayed zinc. Tin, lead, and aluminum have been used considerably. The process is used for structural and tank applications in the field as well as in the shop.

1. According to the above passage, worn bearing surface on shafts are metal-sprayed in order to
    A. prevent corrosion of the shaft
    B. fit them into larger-sized impellers
    C. returns them to their original sizes
    D. replaces worn babbitt metal

    1.____

2. According to the above passage, rotating bearings can be metal-sprayed using
    A. babbitt wire
    B. high-carbon steel
    C. low-carbon steel
    D. any desired metal

    2.____

Questions 3-5.

The method of cleaning which should generally be used is the space assignment method. Under this method, the buildings to be cleaned are divided into different sections. Within each section, each crew of Custodial Assistants is assigned to do one particular cleaning job. For example, within a section, one crew may be assigned to cleaning offices, another to scrubbing floors, a third to collecting trash, and so on. Other methods which may be used are the post-assignment methods and the gang-cleaning method. Under the post-assignment method, a Custodial Assistant is assigned to one area of a building and performs all cleaning jobs in that area. This method is seldom used except where buildings are so small and distant from each other that it is not economical to use the space-assigned method. Under the gang-cleaning method, a Custodial Foreman takes a number of Custodial Assistants through a section of the building. These Custodial Assistants work as a group and complete the various cleaning jobs as they go. This method is generally used only where the building contains very large open areas.

3. According to the above passage, under the space-assignment method, each crew generally
   A. works as a group and does a variety of different cleaning jobs
   B. is assigned to one area and performs all cleaning jobs in that area
   C. does one particular cleaning job within a section of a building
   D. follows the Custodial Foreman through a building containing large, open areas

4. According to the above passage, the post-assignment method is used mostly where the buildings to be cleaned are _____ in size and situated _____.
   A. large; close together
   B. small; close together
   C. large; far apart
   D. small; far apart

5. As used in the above passage, the word *economical* means MOST NEARLY
   A. thrifty
   B. agreed
   C. unusual
   D. wasteful

Questions 6-9.

The desirability of complete refuse collection by municipalities is becoming generally accepted. In many cases, however, such ideal service is economically impractical and certain limits must be imposed. Some municipal authorities find it necessary to regulate the quantity of refuse, by weight or volume, which will be collected from a single residence or place of business at one collection. The purpose of the regulations is twofold: First, to maintain the degree of service rendered on a somewhat uniform basis; and, second, to insure a more or less constant collection from week to week. If left unregulated, careless producers might permit large quantities of refuse to accumulate on their premises over long periods and place abnormal amounts out for collection at irregular intervals, thus upsetting the collection schedule. Regulation is especially applied to large wholesale, industrial, and manufacturing enterprises which, in the great majority of cases, are required to dispose of all or part of their refuse themselves, at their own expense. The maximum quantities permitted by regulation should obviously be sufficient to take care of a normal accumulation at a household over the established interval between regular collections. In commercial districts, the maximum quantity limitations are often fixed on arbitrary bases rather than on normal production.

6. According to the above passage, many municipalities do not have complete refuse collections because
   A. it costs too much
   B. it is difficult to regulate
   C. it is not a municipal function
   D. they don't consider it desirable

7. According to the above passage, regulation by municipalities of the amount of refuse collected per collection from any one place of business does NOT contribute to
   A. accumulation of refuse by careless producers
   B. maintenance of collection schedules
   C. steady collection from one week to the next
   D. uniform service

8. According to the above passage, regulations by municipalities of refuse collection from certain enterprises helps to cut down
   A. accumulation of refuse for private collection
   B. the amount of refuse produced
   C. variation in the volume of refuse produced
   D. variation in collection service

   8.____

9. According to the above passage, municipalities limit the amount of refuse collected in commercial districts on an arbitrary basis rather than on the basis of a normal accumulation. This is probably done because
   A. arbitrary standards are easy to establish and enforce
   B. normal accumulation is different for each district
   C. normal accumulation would require the collection of too much refuse
   D. there is no such thing as a normal accumulation

   9.____

Questions 10-13.

The following passage is adapted from an old office manual:

Modern office methods, geared to ever higher speeds and aimed at ever greater efficiency, are largely the result of the typewriter. The typewriter is a substitute for handwriting and, in the hands of a skilled typist, not only turns out letters and other documents at least three times faster than a penman can do the work, but turns out the greater volume more uniformly and legibly. With the use of carbon paper and onionskin paper, identical copies can be made at the same time.

The typewriter, besides its effect on the conduct of business and government, has had a very important effect on the position of women. The typewriter has done much to bring women into business and government and today there are vastly more women than men typists. Many women have used the keys of the typewriter to climb the ladder to responsible managerial positions.

The typewriter, as its name implies, employs type to make an ink impression on paper. For many years, the manual typewriter was the standard machine used. Today, the electric typewriter is dominant, and completely automatic typewriters are coming into wider use.

The mechanism of the office manual typewriter includes a set of keys arranged systematically in rows; a semicircular frame of type, connected to the keys by levers; the carriage, or paper carrier; a rubber roller, called a platen, against which the type strikes; and an inked ribbon which makes the impression of the type character when the key strikes it.

10. The above passage mentions a number of good features of the combination of a skilled typist and a typewriter. Of the following, the feature which is NOT mentioned in the passage is
    A. speed   B. uniformity   C. reliability   D. legibility

    10.____

11. According to the above passage, a skilled typist can
    A. turn out at least five carbon copies of typed matter
    B. type at least three times faster than a penman can write
    C. type more than 80 words a minute
    D. readily move into a managerial position

    11.____

54

12. According to the above passage, which of the following is NOT part of the mechanism of a manual typewriter?   12.____
    A. Carbon paper   B. Paper carrier
    C. Platen   D. Inked ribbon

13. According to the above passage, the typewriter has helped   13.____
    A. men more than women in business
    B. women in career advancement into management
    C. men and women equally, but women have taken better advantage of it
    D. more women than men, because men generally dislike routine typing work

Questions 14-18.

Reductions in pipe size of a building heating system are made with eccentric fittings and are pitched downward. The ends of mains with gravity return shall be at least 18" above the water line of the boiler. As condensate flows opposite to the steam, run outs are one size larger than the vertical pipe and are pitched upward. In a one-pipe system, an automatic air vent must be provided at each main to relieve air pressure and to let steam enter the radiator. As steam enters the radiator, a *thermal* device causes the vent to close, thereby holding the steam. Steam mains should not be less than two inches in diameter. The end of the steam main should have a minimum size of one-half of its greatest diameter. Small steam systems should be sized for a 2-oz. pressure drop. Large steam systems should be sized for a 4-oz. pressure drop.

14. The word *thermal*, as used in the above passage, means MOST NEARLY   14.____
    A. convector   B. heat   C. instrument   D. current

15. According to the above passage, the one of the following that is one size larger than the vertical pipe is the   15.____
    A. steam main   B. valve   C. water line   D. run out

16. According to the above paragraph, small steam systems should be sized for a pressure drop of _____ oz.   16.____
    A. 2   B. 3   C. 4   D. 5

17. According to the above passage, ends of mains with gravity return shall be AT LEAST   17.____
    A. 18" above the water line of the boiler
    B. one-quarter of the greatest diameter of the main
    C. twice the size of the vertical pipe in the main
    D. 18" above the steam line of the boiler

18. According to the above passage, the one of the following that is provided at each main to relieve air pressure is a(n)   18.____
    A. gravity return   B. convector   C. eccentric   D. vent

Questions 19-21.

The bearings of all electrical equipment should be subjected to careful inspection at scheduled periodic intervals in order to secure maximum life. The newer type of sleeve bearing requires very little attention since the oil does not become contaminated and oil leakage is negligible. Maintenance of the correct oil level is frequently the only upkeep required for years of service with this type of bearing.

19. According to the above passage, the MAIN reason for making periodic inspections of electrical equipment is to
    A. reduce waste of lubricants
    B. prevent injury to operators
    C. make equipment last longer
    D. keeps operators "on their toes"

19._____

20. According to the above passage, the bearings of electrical equipment should be inspected
    A. whenever the equipment isn't working properly
    B. whenever there is time for inspections
    C. at least once a year
    D. at regular times

20._____

21. According to the above passage, when using the newer type of sleeve bearings,
    A. oil leakage is slight
    B. the oil level should be checked every few years
    C. oil leakage is due to carelessness
    D. oil soon becomes dirty

21._____

Questions 22-25.

There is hardly a city in the country that is not short of fire protection in some areas within its boundaries. These municipalities have spread out and have re-shuffled their residential, business, and industrial districts without readjusting the existing protective fire forces; or creating new protection units. Fire stations are still situated according to the needs of earlier times and have not been altered or improved to house modern firefighting equipment. They are neither efficient for carrying out their tasks nor livable for the men who must occupy them.

22. Of the following, the title which BEST describes the central idea of the above passage is:
    A. The Dynamic Nature of Contemporary Society
    B. The Cost of Fire Protection
    C. The Location and Design of Fire Stations
    D. The Design and Use of Firefighting Equipment
    E. The Growth of American Cities

22._____

23. According to the above passage, fire protection is inadequate in the United Sates in
    A. most areas of some cities
    B. some areas of most cities
    C. some areas in all cities
    D. all areas in some cities
    E. most areas in most cities

23._____

24. The one of the following criteria for planning of fire stations which is NOT mentioned in the above passage is:
    A. Comfort of Firemen
    B. Proper Location
    C. Design for Modern Equipment
    D. Efficiency of Operation
    E. Cost of Construction

    24.____

25. Of the following suggestions for improving the fire service, the one which would BEST deal with the problem discussed in the above passage would involve
    A. specialized training in the use of modern fire apparatus
    B. replacement of obsolete fire apparatus
    C. revision of zoning laws
    D. longer basic training for probationary firemen
    E. reassignment of fire districts

    25.____

Questions 26-30.

Stopping, standing, and parking of motor vehicles is regulated by law to keep the public highways open for a smooth flow of traffic, and to keep stopped vehicles from blocking intersections, driveways, signs, fire hydrants, and other areas that must be kept clear. These established regulations apply in all situations, unless otherwise indicated by signs. Other local restrictions are posted in the areas to which they apply. Three examples of these other types of restrictions, which may apply singly or in combination with one another are:
NO STOPPING: This means that a driver may not stop a vehicle for any purpose except when necessary to avoid interference with other vehicles, or in compliance with directions of a police officer or signal.
NO STANDING: This means that a driver may stop a vehicle only temporarily to actually receive or discharge passengers.
NO PARKING: This means that a driver may stop a vehicle only temporarily to actually load or unload merchandise or passengers. When stopped, it is advisable to turn on warning flashers, if equipped with them. However, one should never use a directional signal for this purpose, because it may confuse other drivers. Some NO PARKING signs prohibit parking between certain hours on certain days. For example, the sign may read NO PARKING 8 A.M. to 11 A.M., MONDAY, WEDNESDAY, FRIDAY. These signs are usually utilized on streets where cleaning operations take place on alternate days.

26. The parking regulation that applies to fire hydrants is an example of _____ regulations.
    A. local   B. established   C. posted   D. temporary

    26.____

27. When stopped in a NO PARKING zone, it is advisable to
    A. turn on the right directional signal to indicate to other drivers that you will remain stopped
    B. turn on the left directional signal to indicate to other drivers that you may be leaving the curb after a period of time
    C. turn on the warning flashers if your car is equipped with them
    D. put the vehicle in reverse so that the backup lights will be on to warn approaching cars that you have temporarily stopped

    27.____

28. You may stop a vehicle temporarily to discharge passengers in an area under the restriction of a _____ zone.
    A. NO STOPPING – NO STANDING
    B. NO STANDING – NO PARKING
    C. NO PARKING – NO STOPPING
    D. NO STOPPING – NO STANDING – NO PARKING

29. A sign reads "NO PARKING 8 A.M. to 11 A.M., MONDAY, WEDNESDAY, FRIDAY."
    Based on this sign, an enforcement officer would issue a summons to a car that is parked on a
    A. Tuesday at 9:30 A.M.
    B. Wednesday at 12:00 A.M.
    C. Friday at 10:30 A.M.
    D. Saturday at 8:00 A.M.

30. NO PARKING signs prohibiting parking between certain hours, on certain days, are usually utilized on streets where
    A. vehicles frequently take on and discharge passengers
    B. cleaning operations take place on alternate days
    C. NO STOPPING signs have been ignored
    D. commercial vehicles take on and unload merchandise

KEY (CORRECT ANSWERS)

1.	C	11.	B	21.	A
2.	A	12.	A	22.	C
3.	C	13.	B	23.	B
4.	D	14.	B	24.	E
5.	A	15.	D	25.	E
6.	A	16.	A	26.	B
7.	A	17.	A	27.	C
8.	D	18.	D	28.	B
9.	C	19.	C	29.	C
10.	C	20.	D	30.	B

CLERICAL ABILITIES TEST
EXAMINATION SECTION
TEST 1

DIRECTIONS: Each question or incomplete statement is followed by several suggested answers or completions. Select the one that BEST answers the question or completes the statement. *PRINT THE LETTER OF THE CORRECT ANSWER IN THE SPACE AT THE RIGHT.*

Questions 1-10.

DIRECTIONS: Questions 1 through 10 consist of lines of names, dates, and numbers. For each question, you are to choose the option (A, B, C, or D) in Column II which EXACTLY matches the information in Column I. *PRINT THE LETTER OF THE CORRECT ANSWER IN THE SPACE AT THE RIGHT.*

SAMPLE QUESTION

Column I
Schneider 11/16/75 581932

Column II
A. Schneider 11/16/75 518932
B. Schneider 11/16/75 581932
C. Schnieder 11/16/75 581932
D. Shnieder 11/16/75 518932

The correct answer is B. Only Option B shows the name, date, and number exactly as they are in Column I. Option A has a mistake in the number. Option C has a mistake in the name. Option D has a mistake in the name and in the number. Now answer Questions 1 through 10 in the same manner.

Column I
1. Johnston 12/26/74 659251

Column II
A. Johnson 12/23/74 659251
B. Johston 12/26/74 659251
C. Johnston 12/26/74 695251
D. Johnston 12/26/74 659251

1._____

2. Allison 1/26/75 9939256

A. Allison 1/26/75 9939256
B. Alisson 1/26/75 9939256
C. Allison 1/26/76 9399256
D. Allison 1/26/75 9993356

2._____

3. Farrell 2/12/75 361251

A. Farell 2/21/75 361251
B. Farrell 2/12/75 361251
C. Farrell 2/21/75 361251
D. Farrell 2/12/75 361151

3._____

2 (#1)

4. Guerrero 4/28/72 105689
    A. Guererro 4/28/72 105689
    B. Guererro 4/28/72 105986
    C. Guererro 4/28/72 105869
    D. Guererro 4/28/72 105689
4.____

5. McDonnell 6/05/73 478215
    A. McDonnell 6/15/73 478215
    B. McDonnell 6/05/73 478215
    C. McDonnell 6/05/73 472815
    D. MacDonell 6/05/73 478215
5.____

6. Shepard 3/31/71 075421
    A. Sheperd 3/31/71 075421
    B. Shepard 3/13/71 075421
    C. Shepard 3/31/71 075421
    D. Shepard 3/13/71 075241
6.____

7. Russell 4/01/69 031429
    A. Russell 4/01/69 031429
    B. Russell 4/10/69 034129
    C. Russell 4/10/69 031429
    D. Russell 4/01/69 034129
7.____

8. Phillips 10/16/68 961042
    A. Philipps 10/16/68 961042
    B. Phillips 10/16/68 960142
    C. Phillips 10/16/68 961042
    D. Philipps 10/16/68 916042
8.____

9. Campbell 11/21/72 624856
    A. Campbell 11/21/72 624856
    B. Campbell 11/21/72 624500
    C. Campbell 11/21/72 624686
    D. Campbel 11/21/72 624856
9.____

10. Patterson 9/18/71 76199176
    A. Patterson 9/18/72 76191976
    B. Patterson 9/18/71 76199176
    C. Patterson 9/18/72 76199176
    D. Patterson 9/18/71 76919176
10.____

Questions 11-15.

DIRECTIONS: Questions 11 through 15 consist of groups of numbers and letters which you are to compare. For each question, you are to choose the option (A, B, C, or D) in Column I which EXACTLY matches the group of numbers and letters given in Column I.

SAMPLE QUESTION

Column I
B92466

Column II
A. B92644
B. B94266
C. A92466
D. B92466

The correct answer is D. Only Option D in Column II shows the group of numbers and letters EXACTLY as it appears in Column I. Now answer Questions 11 through 15 in the same manner.

Column I
11. 925AC5

Column II
A. 952CA5
B. 925AC5
C. 952AC5
D. 925CA6

11._____

12. Y006925

A. Y060925
B. Y006295
C. Y006529
D. Y006925

12._____

13. J236956

A. J236956
B. J326965
C. J239656
D. J932656

13._____

14. AB6952

A. AB6952
B. AB9625
C. AB9652
D. AB6925

14._____

15. X259361

A. X529361
B. X259631
C. X523961
D. X259361

15._____

Questions 16-25.

DIRECTIONS: Each of questions 16 through 25 consists of three lines of code letters and three lines of numbers. The numbers on each line should correspond with the code letters on the same line in accordance with the table below.

Code Letter	S	V	W	A	Q	M	X	E	G	K
Corresponding Number	0	1	2	3	4	5	5	7	8	9

On some of the lines, an error exists in the coding. Compare the letters and numbers in each question carefully. If you find an error or errors on:
    only one of the lines in the question, mark your answer A;
    any two lines in the question, mark your answer B;
    all three lines in the question, mark your answer C;
    none of the lines in the question, mark your answer D.

4 (#1)

SAMPLE QUESTION

WQGKSXG	2489068
XEKVQMA	6591453
KMAESXV	9527061

In the above sample, the first line is correct since each code letter listed has the correct corresponding number. On the second line, an error exists because code letter E should have the number 7 instead of the number 5. On the third line, an error exists because the code letter A should have the number 3 instead of the number 2. Since there are errors in two of the three lines, the correct answer is B. Now answer Questions 16 through 25 in the same manner.

16. SWQEKGA   0247983   16.____
      KEAVSXM   9731065
      SSAXGKQ   0036894

17. QAMKMVS   4259510   17.____
      MGGEASX   5897306
      KSWMKWS   9125920

18. WKXQWVE   2964217   18.____
      QKXXQVA   4966413
      AWMXGVS   3253810

19. GMMKASE   8559307   19.____
      AWVSKSW   3210902
      QAVSVGK   4310189

20. XGKQSMK   6894049   20.____
      QSVKEAS   4019730
      GSMXKMV   8057951

21. AEKMWSG   3195208   21.____
      MKQSVQK   5940149
      XGQAEVW   6843712

22. XGMKAVS   6858310   22.____
      SKMAWEQ   0953174
      GVMEQSA   8167403

23. VQSKAVE   1489317   23.____
      WQGKAEM   2489375
      MEGKAWQ   5689324

24. XMQVSKG   6541098   24.____
      QMEKEWS   4579720
      KMEVGKG   9571983

5 (#1)

25. GKVAMEW   88912572   25.____
    AXMVKAE   3651937
    KWAGMAV   9238531

Questions 26-35.

DIRECTIONS: Each of Questions 26 through 35 consists of a column of figures. For each question, add the column of figures and choose the correct answer from the four choices given.

26. 5,665.43   26.____
     2,356.69
     6,447.24
     7,239.65

    A. 20,698.01   B. 21,709.01
    C. 21,718.01   D. 22,609.01

27. 817,209.55   27.____
     264,354.29
      82,368.76
     849,964.89

    A. 1,893.977.49   B. 1,989,988.39
    C. 2,009,077.39   D. 2,013,897.49

28. 156,366.89   28.____
     249,973.23
     823,229.49
      56,869.45

    A. 1,286,439.06   B. 1,287,521.06
    C. 1,297,539.06   D. 1,296,421.06

29.   23,422.15   29.____
     149,696.24
     238,377.53
      86,289.79
     505,533.63

    A. 989,229.34   B. 999,879.34
    C. 1,003,330.34   D. 1,023,329.34

30. 2,468,926.70
     656,842.28
      49,723.15
     832,369.59

    A. 3,218,062.72   B. 3,808,092.72
    C. 4,007,861.72   D. 4,818,192.72

30._____

31.   524,201.52
     7,775,678.51
     8,345,299.63
    40,628,898.08
    31,374,670.07

    A. 88,646,647.81   B. 88,646,747.91
    C. 88,648,647.91   D. 88,648,747.81

31._____

32. 6,824,829.40
      682,482.94
    5,542,015.27
      775,678.51
    7,732,507.25

    A. 21,557,513.37   B. 21,567,513.37
    C. 22,567,503.37   D. 22,567,513.37

32._____

33. 22,109,405.58
     6,097,093.43
     5,050,073.99
     8,118,050.05
     4,313,980.82

    A. 45,688,593.87   B. 45,688,603.87
    C. 45,689,593.87   D. 45,689,603.87

33._____

34. 79,324,114.19
    99,848,129.74
    43,331,653.31
    41,610,207.14

    A. 264,114,104.38   B. 264,114,114.38
    C. 265,114,114.38   D. 265,214,104.38

34._____

35. 33,729,653.94
    5,959,342.58
    26,052,715.47
    4,452,669.52
    7,079,953.59

    A. 76,374,334.10
    B. 76,375,334.10
    C. 77,274,335.10
    D. 77,275,335.10

35.____

Questions 36-40.

DIRECTIONS: Each of Questions 36 through 40 consists of a single number in Column I and four options in Column II. For each question, you are to choose the option (A, B, C, or D) in Column II which EXACTLY matches the number in Column I.

SAMPLE QUESTION

Column I
5965121

Column II
A. 5956121
B. 5965121
C. 5966121
D. 5965211

The correct answer is B. Only Option B shows the number EXACTLY as it appears in Column I. Now answer Questions 36 through 40 in the same manner.

Column I
36. 9643242

Column II
A. 9643242
B. 9462342
C. 9642442
D. 9463242

36.____

37. 3572477

A. 3752477
B. 3725477
C. 3572477
D. 3574277

37.____

38. 5276101

A. 5267101
B. 5726011
C. 5271601
D. 5276101

38.____

39. 4469329

A. 4496329
B. 4469329
C. 4496239
D. 4469239

39.____

40. 2326308
A. 2236308
B. 2233608
C. 2326308
D. 2323608

KEY (CORRECT ANSWERS)

1.	D	11.	B	21.	A	31.	D
2.	A	12.	D	22.	C	32.	A
3.	B	13.	A	23.	B	33.	B
4.	D	14.	A	24.	D	34.	A
5.	B	15.	D	25.	A	35.	C
6.	C	16.	D	26.	B	36.	A
7.	A	17.	C	27.	D	37.	C
8.	C	18.	A	28.	A	38.	D
9.	A	19.	D	29.	C	39.	B
10.	B	20.	B	30.	C	40.	C

TEST 2

DIRECTIONS: Each question or incomplete statement is followed by several suggested answers or completions. Select the one that BEST answers the question or completes the statement. *PRINT THE LETTER OF THE CORRECT ANSWER IN THE SPACE AT THE RIGHT.*

Questions 1-5.

DIRECTIONS: Each of Questions 1 through 5 consists of a name and a dollar amount. In each question, the name and dollar amount in Column II should be an EXACT copy of the name and dollar amount in Column I. If there is:
    a mistake only in the name, mark your answer A;
    a mistake only in the dollar amount, mark your answer B;
    a mistake in both the name and the dollar amount, mark your answer C;
    no mistake in either the name or the dollar amount, mark your answer D.

SAMPLE QUESTION

Column I	Column II
George Peterson	George Petersson
$125.50	$125.50

Compare the name and dollar amount in Column II with the name and dollar amount in Column I. The name *Petersson* in Column II is spelled *Peterson* in Column I. The amount is the same in both columns. Since there is a mistake only in the name, the answer to the sample question is A. Now answer Questions 1 through 5 in the same manner.

	Column I	Column II	
1.	Susanne Shultz $3440	Susanne Schultz $3440	1._____
2.	Anibal P. Contrucci $2121.61	Anibel P. Contrucci $2112.61	2._____
3.	Eugenio Mendoza $12.45	Eugenio Mendozza $12.45	3._____
4.	Maurice Gluckstadt $4297	Maurice Gluckstadt $4297	4._____
5.	John Pampellonne $4656.94	John Pammpellonne $4566.94	5._____

Questions 6-11.

DIRECTIONS: Each of Questions 6 through 11 consist of a set of names and addresses, which you are to compare. In each question, the name and addresses in Column II should be an EXACT copy of the name and address in Column I. If there is:
- a mistake only in the name, mark your answer A;
- a mistake only in the address, mark your answer B;
- a mistake in both the name and address, mark your answer C;
- no mistake in either the name or address, mark your answer D.

SAMPLE QUESTION

Column I	Column II
Michael Filbert	Michael Filbert
456 Reade Street	645 Reade Street
New York, N.Y. 10013	New York, N.Y. 10013

Since there is a mistake only in the address (the street number should be 456 instead of 645), the answer to the sample question is B. Now answer Questions 6 through 11 in the same manner.

	Column I	Column II	
6.	Hilda Goettelmann 55 Lenox Rd. Brooklyn, N.Y. 11226	Hilda Goettelman 55 Lenox Ave. Brooklyn, N.Y. 11226	6.____
7.	Arthur Sherman 2522 Batchelder St. Brooklyn, N.Y. 11235	Arthur Sharman 2522 Batcheder St. Brooklyn, N.Y. 11253	7.____
8.	Ralph Barnett 300 West 28 Street New York, New York 10001	Ralph Barnett 300 West 28 Street New York, New York 10001	8.____
9.	George Goodwin 135 Palmer Avenue Staten Island, New York 10302	George Godwin 135 Palmer Avenue Staten Island, New York 10302	9.____
10.	Alonso Ramirez 232 West 79 Street New York, N.Y. 10024	Alonso Ramirez 223 West 79 Street New York, N.Y. 10024	10.____
11.	Cynthia Graham 149-34 83 Street Howard Beach, N.Y. 11414	Cynthia Graham 149-35 83 Street Howard Beach, N.Y. 11414	11.____

Questions 12-20.

DIRECTIONS: Questions 12 through 20 are problems in subtraction. For each question do the subtraction and select your answer from the four choices given.

12. 232,921.85
    -179,587.68

    A. 52,433.17   B. 52,434.17
    C. 53,334.17   D. 53,343,17

12.____

13. 5,531,876.29
    -3,897,158.36

    A. 1,634,717.93   B. 1,644,718.93
    C. 1,734,717.93   D. 1,7234,718.93

13.____

14. 1,482,658.22
    -937,925.76

    A. 544,633.46   B. 544,732.46
    C. 545,632.46   D. 545,732.46

14.____

15. 937,828.17
    -259,673.88

    A. 678,154.29   B. 679,154.29
    C. 688,155.39   D. 699,155.39

15.____

16. 760,412.38
    -263,465.95

    A. 496,046.43   B. 496,946.43
    C. 496,956.43   D. 497,046.43

16.____

17. 3,203,902.26
    -2,933,087.96

    A. 260,814.30   B. 269,824.30
    C. 270,814.30   D. 270,824.30

17.____

18. 1,023,468.71
    -934,678.88

    A. 88,780.83   B. 88,789.83
    C. 88,880.83   D. 88,889.83

18.____

19. 831,549.47
    -772,814.78

    A. 58,734.69   B. 58,834.69
    C. 59,735.69   D. 59,834.69

20. 6,306,181.74
    -3,617,376.99

    A. 2,687,904.99 B. 2,688,904.99
    C. 2,689,804.99 D. 2,799,905.99

Questions 21-30.

DIRECTIONS: Each of Questions 21 through 30 consists of three lines of code letters and three lines of numbers. The numbers on each line should correspond with the code letters on the same line in accordance with the table below.

Code Letter	J	U	B	T	Y	D	K	R	L	P
Corresponding Number	0	1	2	3	4	5	5	7	8	9

On some of the lines, an error exists in the coding. Compare the letters and numbers in each question carefully. If you find an error or errors on:
  only *one* of the lines in the question, mark your answer A;
  any *two* lines in the question, mark your answer B;
  all *three* lines in the question, mark your answer C;
  none of the lines in the question, mark your answer D.

SAMPLE QUESTION

BJRPYUR   2079417
DTBPYKJ   5328460
YKLDBLT   4685283

In the above sample, the first line is correct since each code letter listed has the correct corresponding number. On the second line, an error exists because code letter P should have the number 9 instead of the number 8. The third line is correct since each code letter listed has the correct corresponding number. Since there is an error in *one* of the three lines, the correct answer is A. Now answer Questions 21 through 30 in the same manner.

21. BYPDTJL   2495308
    PLRDTJU   9815301
    DTJRYLK   5207486

22. RPBYRJK   7934706
    PKTYLBU   9624821
    KDLPJYR   6489047

5 (#2)

23.	TPYBUJR	3942107	23.____
	BYRKPTU	2476931	
	DUKPYDL	5169458	
24.	KBYDLPL	6345898	24.____
	BLRKBRU	2876261	
	JTULDYB	0318542	
25.	LDPYDKR	8594567	25.____
	BDKDRJL	2565708	
	BDRPLUJ	2679810	
26.	PLRLBPU	9858291	26.____
	LPYKRDJ	88936750	
	TDKPDTR	3569527	
27.	RKURPBY	7617924	27.____
	RYUKPTJ	7426930	
	RTKPTJD	7369305	
28.	DYKPBJT	5469203	28.____
	KLPJBTL	6890238	
	TKPLBJP	3698209	
29.	BTPRJYL	2397148	29.____
	LDKUTYR	8561347	
	YDBLRPJ	4528190	
30.	ULPBKYT	1892643	30.____
	KPDTRBJ	6953720	
	YLKJPTB	4860932	

KEY (CORRECT ANSWERS)

1.	A	11.	D	21.	B
2.	C	12.	C	22.	C
3.	A	13.	A	23.	D
4.	D	14.	B	24.	B
5.	C	15.	A	25.	A
6.	C	16.	B	26.	C
7.	C	17.	C	27.	A
8.	D	18.	B	28.	D
9.	A	19.	A	29.	B
10.	B	20.	B	30.	D

NAME AND NUMBER CHECKING
EXAMINATION SECTION
TEST 1

DIRECTIONS: This test is designed to measure your speed/and accuracy. You are urged to work both quickly and accurately and to do correctly as many lists as you can in the time allowed. The test consists of lists or pairs of names and numbers. Count the number of IDENTICAL pairs in each list. Then, select the correct number, 1, 2, 3, 4, 5, and indicate your choice in the space at the right. Two sample questions are presented for your guidance, together with the correct solutions.

SAMPLE LIST A
Adelphi College – Adelphia College
Braxton Corp – Braxeton Corp.
Wassaic State School – Wassaic State School
Central Islip State Hospital – Central Isllip State Hospital
Greenwich House – Greenwich House

NOTE: There are only two correct pairs—Wassaic State School and Greenwich House. Therefore, the CORRECT answer is 2.

SAMPLE LIST B
78453694 – 78453684
784530 – 784530
533 – 534
67845 – 67845
2368745 – 2368755

NOTE: There are only two correct pairs—784530 and 67845. Therefore, the CORRECT answer is 2.

LIST 1   1.____
    Diagnostic Clinic   – Diagnostic Clinic
    Yorkville Health   – Yorkville Health
    Meinhard Clinic   – Meinhart Clinic
    Corlears Clinic   – Carlears Clinic
    Tremont Diagnostic – Tremont Diagnostic

LIST 2   2.____
    73526   – 73526
    7283627198   – 7283627198
    627   – 637
    728352617283 – 7283526178282
    6281   – 6281

2 (#1)

LIST 3   3.____
- Jefferson Clinic — Jeffersen Clinic
- Mott Haven Center — Mott Havan Center
- Bronx Hospital — Bronx Hospital
- Montefiore Hospital — Montifeore Hospital
- Beth Isreal Hospital — Beth Israel Hospital

LIST 4   4.____
- 936271826 — 936371826
- 5271 — 5291
- 82637192037 — 82637192037
- 527182 — 5271882
- 726354256 — 72635456

LIST 5   5.____
- Trinity Hospital — Trinity Hospital
- Central Harlem — Centrel Harlem
- St. Luke's Hospital — St. Lukes' Hospital
- Mt. Sinai Hospital — Mt. Sinia Hospital
- N.Y. Dispensery — N.Y. Dispensary

LIST 6   6.____
- 725361552637 — 725361555637
- 7526378 — 7526377
- 6975 — 6975
- 82637481028 — 82637481028
- 3427 — 3429

LIST 7   7.____
- Misericordia Hospital — Miseracordia Hospital
- Lebonan Hospital — Lebanon Hospital
- Gouverneur Hospital — Gouverner Hospital
- German Polyclinic — German Policlinic
- French Hospital — French Hospital

LIST 8   8.____
- 8277364933251 — 827364933351
- 63728 — 63728
- 367281 — 367281
- 62733846273 — 6273846293
- 62836 — 6283

LIST 9   9.____
- King's County Hospital — Kings County Hospital
- St. Johns Long Island — St. John's Long Island
- Bellevue Hospital — Bellvue Hospital
- Beth David Hospital — Beth David Hospital
- Samaritan Hospital — Samariton Hospital

LIST 10
 62836454   – 62836455
 42738267   – 42738369
 573829   – 573829
 738291627874   – 738291627874
 725   - 735

10.____

LIST 11
 Bloomingdal Clinic   – Bloomingdale Clinic
 Communitty Hospital   – Community Hospital
 Metroplitan Hospital   – Metropoliton Hospital
 Lenox Hill Hospital   – Lonex Hill Hospital
 Lincoln Hospital   – Lincoln Hospital

11.____

LIST 12
 6283364728   – 6283648
 627385   – 627383
 54283902   – 54283602
 63354   – 63354
 7283562781   - 7283562781

12.____

LIST 13
 Sydenham Hospital   – Sydanham Hospital
 Roosevalt Hospital   – Roosevelt Hospital
 Vanderbilt Clinic   – Vanderbild Clinic
 Women's Hospital   – Woman's Hospital
 Flushing Hospital   – Flushing Hospital

13.____

LIST 14
 62738   – 62738
 727355542321   – 72735542321
 263849332   – 263849332
 262837   – 263837
 47382912   - 47382922

14.____

LIST 15
 Episcopal Hospital   – Episcapal Hospital
 Flower Hospital   – Flouer Hospital
 Stuyvesent Clinic   – Stuyvesant Clinic
 Jamaica Clinic   – Jamaica Clinic
 Ridgwood Clinic   – Ridgewood Clinic

15.____

LIST 16
 628367299   – 628367399
 111   – 111
 118293304829   – 1182839489
 4448   – 4448
 333693678   - 333693678

16.____

LIST 17
- Arietta Crane Farm — Areitta Crane Farm
- Bikur Chilim Home — Bikur Chilom Home
- Burke Foundation — Burke Foundation
- Blythedale Home — Blythdale Home
- Campbell Cottages — Cambell Cottages

17.____

LIST 18
- 32123 — 32132
- 273893326783 — 27389326783
- 473829 — 473829
- 7382937 — 7383937
- 3628890122332 — 36289012332

18.____

LIST 19
- Caraline Rest — Caroline Rest
- Loreto Rest — Loretto Rest
- Edgewater Creche — Edgwater Creche
- Holiday Farm — Holiday Farm
- House of St. Giles — House of st. Giles

19.____

LIST 20
- 557286777 — 55728677
- 3678902 — 3678892
- 1567839 — 1567839
- 7865434712 — 7865344712
- 9927382 — 9927382

20.____

LIST 21
- Isabella Home — Isabela Home
- James A. Moore Home — James A. More Home
- The Robin's Nest — The Roben's Nest
- Pelham Home — Pelam Home
- St. Eleanora's Home — St. Eleanora's Home

21.____

LIST 22
- 273648293048 — 273648293048
- 334 — 334
- 7362536478 — 7362536478
- 7362819273 — 7362819273
- 7362 — 7363

22.____

LIST 23
- St. Pheobe's Mission — St. Phebe's Mission
- Seaside Home — Seaside Home
- Speedwell Society — Speedwell Society
- Valeria Home — Valera Home
- Wiltwyck — Wildwyck

23.____

5 (#1)

LIST 24   24.____
    63728   – 63738
    63728192736   – 63728192738
    428   – 458
    62738291527   – 62738291529
    63728192   - 63728192

LIST 25   25.____
    McGaffin   – McGafin
    David Ardslee   – David Ardslee
    Axton Supply   – Axeton Supply Co
    Alice Russell   – Alice Russell
    Dobson Mfg. Co.   – Dobsen Mfg. Co.

KEY (CORRECT ANSWERS)

1.	3	11.	1
2.	3	12.	2
3.	1	13.	1
4.	1	14.	2
5.	1	15.	1
6.	2	16.	3
7.	1	17.	1
8.	2	18.	1
9.	1	19.	1
10.	2	20.	2

21. 1
22. 4
23. 2
24. 1
25. 2

TEST 2

DIRECTIONS: This test is designed to measure your speed/and accuracy. You are urged to work both quickly and accurately and to do correctly as many lists as you can in the time allowed. The test consists of lists or pairs of names and numbers. Count the number of IDENTICAL pairs in each list. Then, select the correct number, 1, 2, 3, 4, 5, and indicate your choice in the space at the right.

LIST 1
    82637381028   – 82637281028
    928   – 928
    72937281028   – 72937281028
    7362   – 7362
    927382615   – 927382615

1.____

LIST 2
    Albee Theatre   – Albee Theatre
    Lapland Lumber Co.   – Laplund Lumber Co.
    Adelphi College   – Adelphi College
    Jones & Son Inc.   – Jones & Sons Inc.
    S.W. Ponds Co.   – S.W. Ponds Co.

2.____

LIST 3
    85345   – 85345
    895643278   – 895643277
    726352   – 726353
    632685   – 632685
    7263524   – 7236524

3.____

LIST 4
    Eagle Library   – Eagle Library
    Dodge Ltd.   – Dodge Co.
    Stromberg Carlson   – Stromberg Carlsen
    Clairice Ling   – Clairice Linng
    Mason Book Co.   – Matson Book Co.

4.____

LIST 5
    66273   – 66273
    629   – 629
    7382517283   – 7382517283
    637281   – 639281
    2738261   – 2788261

5.____

LIST 6
    Robert MacColl   – Robert McColl
    Buick Motor   – Buck Motors
    Murray Bay & Co. Ltd. – Murray Bay Co. Ltd.
    L.T. Ltyle   – L.T. Lyttle
    A.S. Landas   – A.S. Landas

6.____

LIST 7
		7.____
6271526374890	– 627152637490	
73526189	– 73526189	
5372	– 5392	
637281142	– 63728124	
4783946	– 4783046	

LIST 8
8.____

- Tyndall Burke — Tyndell Burke
- W. Briehl — W. Briehl
- Burritt Publishing Co. — Buritt Publishing Co.
- Frederick Breyer & Co. — Frederick Breyer Co.
- Bailey Buulard — Bailey Bullard

LIST 9
9.____

- 634 — 634
- 16837 — 163837
- 273892223678 — 27389223678
- 527182 — 527782
- 3628901223 — 3629002223

LIST 10
10.____

- Ernest Boas — Ernest Boas
- Rankin Barne — Rankin Barnes
- Edward Appley — Edward Appely
- Camel — Camel
- Caiger Food Co. — Caiger Food Co.

LIST 11
11.____

- 6273 — 6273
- 322 — 332
- 15672839 — 15672839
- 63728192637 — 63728192639
- 738 — 738

LIST 12
12.____

- Wells Fargo Co. — Wells Fargo Co.
- W.D. Brett — W.D. Britt
- Tassco Co. — Tassko Co.
- Republic Mills — Republic Mill
- R.W. Burnham — R.W. Burhnam

LIST 13
13.____

- 7253529152 — 7283529152
- 6283 — 6383
- 52839102738 — 5283910238
- 308 — 398
- 82637201927 — 8263720127

LIST 14
    Schumacker Co.   – Shumacker Co.
    C.H. Caiger   – C.H. Caiger
    Abraham Strauss   – Abram Straus
    B.F. Boettjer   – B.F. Boettijer
    Cut-Rate Store   – Cut-Rate Stores

14.____

LIST 15
    15273826   – 15273826
    72537   – 73537
    726391027384   – 62639107384
    637389   – 627399
    725382910   – 725382910

15.____

LIST 16
    Hixby Ltd.   – Hixby Lt'd.
    S. Reiner   – S. Riener
    Reynard Co.   – Reynord Co.
    Esso Gassoline Co.   – Esso Gasolene Co.
    Belle Brock   – Belle Brock

16.____

LIST 17
    7245   – 7245
    819263728192   – 819263728172
    682537289   – 682537298
    789   – 789
    82936542891   – 82936542891

17.____

LIST 18
    Joseph Cartwright   – Joseph Cartwrite
    Foote Food Co.   – Foot Food Co.
    Weiman & Held   – Weiman & Held
    Sanderson Shoe Co. – Sandersen Shoe Co.
    A.M. Byrne   – A.N. Byrne

18.____

LIST 19
    4738267   – 4738277
    63728   – 63729
    6283628901   – 6283628991
    918264   – 918264
    263728192037   – 2637728192073

19.____

LIST 20
    Exray Laboratories   – Exray Labratories
    Curley Toy Co.   – Curly Toy Co.
    J. Lauer & Cross   – J. Laeur & Cross
    Mireco Brands   – Mireco Brands
    Sandor Lorand   – Sandor Larand

20.____

4 (#2)

LIST 21   21.____
   607   – 609
   6405   – 6403
   976   – 996
   101267   – 101267
   2065432   – 20965432

LIST 22   22.____
   John Macy & Sons   – John Macy & Son
   Venus Pencil Co.   – Venus Pencil Co.
   Nell McGinnis   – Nell McGinnis
   McCutcheon & Co.   – McCutcheon & Co.
   Sun-Tan Oil   – Sun-Tan Oil

LIST 23   23.____
   703345700   – 703345700
   46754   – 466754
   3367490   – 3367490
   3379   – 3778
   47384   – 47394

LIST 24   24.____
   arthritis   – arthritis
   asthma   – asthma
   endocrine   – endocrene
   gastro-enterological – gastrol-enteralogical
   orthopedic   – orthopedic

LIST 25   25.____
   743829432   – 743828432
   998   – 998
   732816253902   – 732816252902
   46829   – 46830
   7439120249   – 7439210249

KEY (CORRECT ANSWERS)

1.	4		11.	3
2.	3		12.	1
3.	2		13.	1
4.	1		14.	1
5.	2		15.	2
6.	1		16.	1
7.	2		17.	3
8.	1		18.	1
9.	1		19.	1
10.	3		20.	1

21. 1
22. 4
23. 2
24. 3
25. 1

CODING

COMMENTARY

An ingenious question-type called coding, involving elements of alphabetizing, filing, name and number comparison, and evaluative judgment and application, has currently won wide acceptance in testing circles for measuring clerical aptitude and general ability, particularly on the senior (middle) grades (levels).

While the directions for this question usually vary in detail, the candidate is generally asked to consider groups of names, codes, and numbers, and, then, according to a given plan, to arrange codes in alphabetic order; to arrange these in numerical sequence; to re-arrange columns of names and numbers in correct order; to espy errors in coding; to choose the correct coding arrangement in consonance with the given directions and examples, etc.

This question-type appears to have few paramaters in respect to form, substance, or degree of difficulty.

Accordingly, acquaintance with, and practice in, the coding question is recommended for the serious candidate.

EXAMINATION SECTION
TEST 1

DIRECTIONS:

CODE TABLE

Name of Applicant	H A N G S B R U K E
Test Code	c o m p l e x i t y
File Number	0 1 2 3 4 5 6 7 8 9

Assume that each of the above *capital letters* is the first letter of the Name of an Applicant, that the *small letter* directly beneath each capital letter is the Test Code for the Applicant, and that the *number* directly beneath each code letter is the File Number for the Applicant.

In each of the following questions, the test code letters and the file numbers in Columns 2 and 3 should correspond to the capital letters in Column 1. For each question, look at each column carefully and mark your answer as follows:

If there is an error only in Column 2, mark your answer A.
If there is an error only in Column 3, mark your answer B.
If there is an error in both Columns 2 and 3, mark your answer C.
If both Columns 2 and 3 are correct, mark your answer D.

The following sample question is given to help you understand the procedure.

SAMPLE QUESTION

Column 1	Column 2	Column 3
AKEHN	otyci	18902

2 (#1)

In Column 2, the final test code letter "i" should be "m." Column 3 is correctly coded to Column 1. Since there is an error only in Column 2, the answer is A

	Column 1	Column 2	Column 3	
1.	NEKKU	mytti	29987	1.___
2.	KRAEB	txlye	86095	2.___
3.	ENAUK	ymoit	92178	3.___
4.	REANA	xeomo	69121	4.___
5.	EKHSE	ytcxy	97049	5.___

KEY (CORRECT ANSWERS)

1. B
2. C
3. D
4. A
5. C

TEST 2

DIRECTIONS: The employee identification codes in Column I begin and end with a capital letter and have an eight-digit number in between. In Questions 1 through 8, employee identification codes in Column I are to be arranged according to the following rules:

First: Arrange in alphabetical order according to the first letter.

Second: When two or more employee identification codes have the same first letter, arrange in alphabetical order according to the last letter.

Third: When two or more employee codes have the same first and last letters, arrange in numerical order beginning with the lowest number.

The employee identification codes in Column I are numbered 1 through 5 in the order in which they are listed. In Column II the numbers 1 through 5 are arranged in four different ways to show different arrangements of the corresponding employee identification numbers. Choose the answer in Column II in which the employee identification numbers are arranged according to the above rules.

SAMPLE QUESTION

Column I
1. E75044127B
2. B96399104A
3. B93939086A
4. B47064465H
5. B99040922A

Column II
A. 4, 1, 3, 2, 5
B. 4, 1, 2, 3, 5
C. 4, 3, 2, 5, 1
D. 3, 2, 5, 4, 1

In the sample question, the four employee identification codes starting with B should be put before the employee identification code starting with E. The employee identification codes starting with B and ending with A should be put before the employee identification codes starting with B and ending with H. The three employee identification codes starting with B and ending with A should be listed in numerical order, beginning with the lowest number. The correct way to arrange the employee identification codes, therefore, is 3, 2, 5, 4, 1 shown below.

3. B93939086A
2. B96399104A
5. B99040922A
4. B47064465H
1. E75044127B

Therefore, the answer to the sample question is D. Now answer the following questions according to the above rules.

Column I
1. 1. G42786441J
   2. H45665413J
   3. G43117690J
   4. G435466981
   5. G416799421

Column II
A. 2, 5, 4, 3, 1
B. 5, 4, 1, 3, 2
C. 4, 5, 1, 3, 2
D. 1, 3, 5, 4, 2

1._____

2 (#2)

2.
1. S44556178T
2. T43457169T
3. S53321176T
4. T53317998S
5. S67673942S

A. 1, 3, 5, 2, 4
B. 4, 3, 5, 2, 1
C. 5, 3, 1, 2, 4
D. 5, 1, 3, 4, 2

2. _____

3.
1. R63394217D
2. R63931247D
3. R53931247D
4. R66874239D
4. R46799366D

A. 5, 4, 2, 3, 1
B. 1, 5, 3, 2, 4
C. 5, 3, 1, 2, 4
D. 5, 1, 2, 3, 4

3. _____

4.
1. A35671968B
2. A35421794C
3. A35466987B
4. C10435779A
5. C00634779B

A. 3, 2, 1, 4, 5
B. 2, 3, 1, 5, 4
C. 1, 3, 2, 4, 5
D. 3, 1, 2, 4, 5

4. _____

5.
1. I99746426Q
2. I10445311Q
3. J63749877P
4. J03421739Q
5. J00765311Q

A. 2, 1, 3, 5, 4
B. 5, 4, 2, 1, 3
C. 4, 5, 3, 2, 1
D. 2, 1, 4, 5, 3

5. _____

6.
1. M33964217N
2. N33942770N
3. N06155881M
4. M00433669M
5. M79034577N

A. 4, 1, 5, 2, 3
B. 5, 1, 4, 3, 2
C. 4, 1, 5, 3, 2
D. 1, 4, 5, 2, 3

6. _____

7.
1. D77643905C
2. D44106788C
3. D13976022F
4. D97655430E
5. D00439776F

A. 1, 2, 5, 3, 4
B. 5, 3, 2, 1, 4
C. 2, 1, 5, 3, 4
D. 2, 1, 4, 5, 3

7. _____

8.
1. W22746920A
2. W22743720A
3. W32987655A
4. W43298765A
5. W30987433A

A. 2, 1, 3, 4, 5
B. 2, 1, 5, 3, 4
C. 1, 2, 3, 4, 5
D. 1, 2, 5, 3, 4

8. _____

KEY (CORRECT ANSWERS)

1. B   5. A
2. D   6. C
3. C   7. D
4. D   8. B

TEST 3

DIRECTIONS: Each of the following equations consists of three sets of names and name codes. In each question, the two names and name codes on the same line are supposed to be exactly the same.

Look carefully at each set of names and codes and mark your answer:
- A. if there are mistakes in all three sets
- B. if there are mistakes in two of the sets
- C. if there is a mistake in only one set
- D. if there are no mistakes in any of the sets

The following sample question is given to help you understand the procedure.

Macabe, John N.	- V	53162	Macade, John N.	- V	53162
Howard, Joan S.	- J	24791	Howard, Joan S.	- J	24791
Ware, Susan B.	- A	45068	Ware, Susan B.	- A	45968

In the above sample question, the names and name codes of the first set are not exactly the same because of the spelling of the last name (Macabe - Macade). The names and name codes of the second set are exactly the same. The names and name codes of the third set are not exactly the same because the two name codes are different (A 45068 - A 45968), Since there are mistakes in only 2 of the sets, the answer to the sample question is B.

1. Powell, Michael C. - 78537 F   Powell, Michael C. - 78537 F   1.____
   Martinez, Pablo, J. - 24435 P   Martinez, Pablo J. - 24435 P
   MacBane, Eliot M. - 98674 E   MacBane, Eliot M. - 98674 E

2. Fitz-Kramer Machines Inc. - 259090   Fitz-Kramer Machines Inc. - 259090   2.____
   Marvel Cleaning Service - 482657   Marvel Cleaning Service - 482657
   Donate, Carl G. - 637418   Danato, Carl G. - 687418

3. Martin Davison Trading Corp. - 43108 T   Martin Davidson Trading Corp. - 43108 T   3.____
   Cotwald Lighting Fixtures - 76065 L   Cotwald Lighting Fixtures - 70056 L
   R. Crawford Plumbers - 23157 C   R. Crawford Plumbers - 23157 G

4. Fraiman Engineering Corp. - M4773   Friaman Engineering Corp. -M4773   4.____
   Neuman, Walter B. - N7745   Neumen, Walter B. - N7745
   Pierce, Eric M. - W6304   Pierce, Eric M. - W6304

5. Constable, Eugene - B 64837   Comstable, Eugene - B 64837   5.____
   Derrick, Paul - H 27119   Derrik, Paul - H 27119
   Heller, Karen - S 49606   Heller, Karen - S 46906

6. Hernando Delivery Service Co. - D 7456   Hernando Delivery Service Co. - D 7456   6.____
   Barettz Electrical Supplies - N 5392   Barettz Electrical Supplies - N 5392
   Tanner, Abraham - M 4798   Tanner, Abraham - M 4798

7. Kalin Associates - R 38641   Kaline Associates - R 38641   7.____
   Sealey, Robert E. - P 63533   Sealey, Robert E. - P 63553
   Scalsi Office Furniture   Scalsi Office Furniture

2 (#3)

8. Janowsky, Philip M.- 742213　　　　Janowsky, Philip M.- 742213　　　　　　8._____
   Hansen, Thomas H. - 934816　　　　　Hanson, Thomas H. - 934816
   L. Lester and Son Inc. - 294568　　　L. Lester and Son Inc. - 294568

KEY (CORRECT ANSWERS)

1. D
2. C
3. A
4. B
5. A

6. D
7. B
8. C

TEST 4

DIRECTIONS: The following questions are to be answered on the basis of the following Code Table. In this table, for each number, a corresponding code letter is given. Each of the questions contains three pairs of numbers and code letters. In each pair, the code letters should correspond with the numbers in accordance with the Code Table.

CODE TABLE

Number	1	2	3	4	5	6	7	8	9	0
Corresponding Code Letter	Y	N	Z	X	W	T	U	P	S	R

In some of the pairs below, an error exists in the coding. Examine the pairs in each question carefully. If an error exists in:
  Only one of the pairs in the question, mark your answer A.
  Any two pairs in the question, mark your answer B.
  All three pairs in the question, mark your answer C.
  None of the pairs in the question, mark your answer D.

SAMPLE QUESTION

```
37258    -  ZUNWP
948764   -  SXPTTX
73196    -  UZYSP
```

In the above sample, the first pair is correct since each number, as listed, has the correct corresponding code letter. In the second pair, an error exists because the number 7 should have the code letter U instead of the letter T. In the third pair, an error exists because the number 6 should have the code letter T instead of the letter P. Since there are errors in two of the three pairs, the correct answer is B.

1. 493785   - XSZUPW
   86398207 - PTUSPNRU
   5943162   - WSXZYTN

2. 5413968412 - WXYZSTPXYR
   8763451297 - PUTZXWYZSU
   4781965302 - XUPYSUWZRN

3. 79137584 - USYRUWPX
   638247   - TZPNXS
   49679312 - XSTUSZYN

4. 37854296 - ZUPWXNST
   09183298 - RSYXZNSP
   91762358 - SYUTNXWP

5. 3918762485 - ZSYPUTNXPW
   1578291436 - YWUPNSYXZT
   2791385674 - NUSYZPWTUX

2 (#4)

6. 197546821 - YSUWSTPNY   6.____
   873024867 - PUZRNWPTU
   583179246 - WPZYURNXT

7. 510782463 - WYRUSNXTZ   7.____
   478192356 - XUPYSNZWT
   961728532 - STYUNPWXN

KEY (CORRECT ANSWERS)

1. A
2. C
3. B
4. B
5. D

6. C
7. B

TEST 5

DIRECTIONS: Assume that each of the capital letters is the first letter of the name of a city using EAM equipment. The number directly beneath each capital letter is the code number for the city. The small letter beneath each code number is the code letter for the number of EAM divisions in the city and the + or - symbol directly beneath each code letter is the code symbol which signifies whether or not the city uses third generation computers with the EAM equipment.

The questions that follow show City Letters in Column I, Code Numbers in Column II, Code Letters in Column III, and Code Symbols in Column IV. If correct. each City Letter in Column I should correspond by position with each of the three codes shown in the other three columns, in accordance with the coding key shown. BUT there are some errors. For each question,

If there is a total of ONE error in Columns 2, 3, and 4, mark your answer A.
If there is a total of TWO errors in Columns 2, 3, and 4, mark your answer B.
If there is a total of THREE errors in Columns 2, 3, and 4, mark your answer C.
If Columns 2, 3, and 4 are correct, mark your answer D.

SAMPLE QUESTION

I	II	III	IV
City Letter	Code Numbers	Code Letters	Code Symbols
Y J M O S	5 3 7 9 8	e b g i h	- - + + -

The errors are as follows: In Column 2, the Code Number should be "2" instead of "3" for City Letter "J," and in Column 4 the Code Symbol should be "+" instead of "-" for City Letter "Y." Since there is a total of two errors in Columns 2, 3, and 4, the answer to this sample question is B.

Now answer questions 1 through 9 according to these rules.

CODING KEY

City Letter	P	J	R	T	Y	K	M	S	O
Code Number	1	2	3	4	5	6	7	8	9
Code Letter	a	b	c	d	e	f	g	h	i
Code Symbol	+	-	+	-	+	-	+	-	+

	I City Letters	II Code Numbers	III Code Letters	IV Code Symbols	
1.	KORMP	69371	fiega	- - + + +	1.____
2.	OTPSY	94186	bdahe	+ - - - +	2.____
3.	RSJTM	38147	chbeg	- - - - +	3.____
4.	PMSKJ	17862	aghfb	+ + - - -	4.____
5.	MYTJR	75423	gedfc	+ + - - +	5.____
6.	TPKYO	41679	dafei	- + - + -	6.____
7.	SKORT	86935	hficd	- - + + -	7.____
8.	JRYPK	23519	bdeaf	- + + + -	8.____
9.	ROMPY	49715	cigad	+ + - + +	9.____

KEY (CORRECT ANSWERS)

1. B
2. C
3. C
4. D
5. A

6. B
7. A
8. B
9. C

———

TEST 6

Assume that each of the capital letters is the first letter of the name of an offense, that the small letter directly beneath each capital letter is the code letter for the offense, and that the number directly beneath each code letter is the file number for the offense.

DIRECTIONS: In each of the following questions, the code letters and file numbers should correspond to the capital letters.

If there is an error only in Column 2, mark your answer A.
If there is an error only in Column 3, mark your answer B.
If there is an error in both Column 2 and Column 3, mark your answer C.
If both Columns 2 and 3 are correct, mark your answer D.

SAMPLE QUESTION

Column 1	Column 2	Column 3
BNARGHSVVU	emoxtylcci	6357905118

The code letters in Column 2 are correct but the first "5" in Column 3 should be "2." Therefore, the answer is B. Now answer the following questions according to the above rules.

CODE TABLE

Name of Offense	V	A	N	D	S	B	R	U	G	H
Code Letter	c	o	m	p	l	e	x	i	t	y
File Number	1	2	3	4	5	6	7	8	9	0

	Column 1	Column 2	Column 3	
1.	HGDSBNBSVR	ytplxmelcx	0945736517	1.____
2.	SDGUUNHVAH	lptiimycoy	5498830120	2.____
3.	BRSNAAVUDU	exlmooctpi	6753221848	3.____
4.	VSRUDNADUS	cleipmopil	1568432485	4.____
5.	NDSHVRBUAG	mplycxeiot	3450175829	5.____
6.	GHUSNVBRDA	tyilmcexpo	9085316742	6.____
7.	DBSHVURANG	pesycixomt	4650187239	7.____
8.	RHNNASBDGU	xymnolepti	7033256398	8.____

KEY (CORRECT ANSWERS)

1. C
2. D
3. A
4. C
5. B

6. D
7. A
8. C

TEST 7

DIRECTIONS: Each of the following questions contains three sets of code letters and code numbers. In each set, the code numbers should correspond with the code letters as given in the Table, but there is a coding error in some of the sets. Examine the sets in each question carefully.

Mark your answer A if there is a coding error in only ONE of the sets in the question.
Mark your answer B if there is a coding error in any TWO of the sets in the question.
Mark your answer C if there is a coding error in all THREE sets in the question.
Mark your answer D if there is a coding error in NONE of the sets in the question.

SAMPLE QUESTION
fgzduwaf - 35720843
uabsdgfw - 04262538
hhfaudgs - 99340257

In the above sample question, the first set is right because each code number matches the code letter as in the Code Table. In the second set, the corresponding number for the code letter b is wrong because it should be 1 instead of 2. In the third set, the corresponding number for the last code letter s is wrong because it should be 6 instead of 7. Since there is an error in two of the sets, the answer to the above sample question is B.

In the Code Table below, each code letter has a corresponding code number directly beneath it.

CODE TABLE

Code Letter	b	d	f	a	g	s	z	w	h	u
Code Number	1	2	3	4	5	6	7	8	9	0

1. fsbughwz - 36104987   zwubgasz - 78025467   1._____
   ghgufddb - 59583221

2. hafgdaas - 94351446   ddsfabsd - 22734162   2._____
   wgdbssgf - 85216553

3. abfbssbd - 41316712   ghzfaubs - 59734017   3._____
   sdbzfwza - 62173874

4. whfbdzag - 89412745   daaszuub - 24467001   4._____
   uzhfwssd - 07936623

5. zbadgbuh - 71425109   dzadbbsz - 27421167   5._____
   gazhwaff - 54798433

6. fbfuadsh - 31304265   gzfuwzsb - 57300671   6._____
   bashhgag - 14699535

KEY (CORRECT ANSWERS)

1. B
2. C
3. B
4. B
5. D
6. C

———

TEST 8

DIRECTIONS: The following questions are to be answered on the basis of the following Code Table. In this table every letter has a corresponding code number to be punched. Each question contains three pairs of letters and code numbers. In each pair, the code numbers should correspond with the letters in accordance with the Code Table.

```
                  CODE TABLE
Letter            P  L  A  N  D  C  O  B  U  R
Corresponding     1  2  3  4  5  6  7  8  9  0
Code Number
```

In some of the pairs below, an error exists in the coding. Examine the pairs in each question. Mark your answer

- A if there is a mistake in only *one* of the pairs
- B if there is a mistake in only *two* of the pairs
- C if there is a mistake in *all three* of the pairs
- D if there is a mistake in *none* of the pairs

SAMPLE QUESTION

LCBPUPAB - 26819138
ACOABOL   - 3683872
NDURONUC - 46901496

In the above sample, the first pair is correct since each letter as listed has the correct corresponding code number. In the second pair, an error exists because the letter 0 should have the code number 7, instead of 8. In the third pair, an error exists because the letter D should have the code number 5, instead of 6. Since there are errors in two of the three pairs, your answer should be B.

1. ADCANPLC - 35635126   DORURBBO - 57090877   1.____
    PNACBUCP - 14368061

2. LCOBLRAP - 26782931   UPANUPCD - 91349156   2.____
    RLDACLRO - 02536207

3. LCOROPAR - 26707130   BALANRUP - 83234091   3.____
    DOPOAULL - 57173922

4. ONCRUBAP - 74609831   DCLANORD - 56243705   4.____
    AORPDUR - 3771590

5. PANRBUCD - 13408965   UAOCDPLR - 93765120   5.____
    OPDDOBRA - 71556803

6. BAROLDCP - 83072561   PNOCOBLA - 14767823   6.____
    BURPDOLA - 89015723

7. ANNCPABO - 34461387   DBALDRCP - 58325061   7.____
    ACRPOUL - 3601792

97

8. BLAPOUR - 8321790   NOACNPL - 4736412   8.____
   RODACORD - 07536805

9. ADUBURCL - 3598062   NOCOBAPR - 47578310   9.____
   PRONDALU - 10754329

10. UBADCLOR - 98356270   NBUPPARA - 48911033   10.____
    LONDUPRC - 27459106

KEY (CORRECT ANSWERS)

1. C
2. B
3. D
4. B
5. A

6. D
7. B
8. B
9. C
10. A

1. D
2. B

2 (#9)

3.	(1)	H32548137E		A.	2,	4,	5,	1,	3
	(2)	H35243178A		B.	1,	5,	2,	3,	4
	(3)	H35284378F		C.	1,	5,	2,	4,	3
	(4)	H35288337A		D.	2,	1,	5,	3,	4
	(5)	H32883173B							
4.	(1)	K24165039H		A.	4,	2,	5,	3,	1
	(2)	F24106599A		B.	2,	3,	4,	1,	5
	(3)	L21406639G		C.	4,	2,	5,	1,	3
	(4)	C24156093A		D.	1,	3,	4,	5,	2
	(5)	K24165593D							
5.	(1)	H79110642E		A.	2,	1,	3,	5,	4
	(2)	H79101928E		B.	2,	1,	4,	5,	3
	(3)	A79111567F		C.	3,	5,	2,	1,	4
	(4)	H79111796E		D.	4,	3,	5,	1,	2
	(5)	A79111618F							
6.	(1)	P16388385W		A.	3,	4,	5,	2,	1
	(2)	R16388335V		B.	2,	3,	4,	5,	1
	(3)	P16383835W		C.	2,	4,	3,	1,	5
	(4)	R18386865V		D.	3,	1,	5,	2,	4
	(5)	P18686865W							
7.	(1)	B42271749G		A.	4,	1,	5,	2,	3
	(2)	B42271779G		B.	4,	1,	2,	5,	3
	(3)	E43217779G		C.	1,	2,	4,	5,	3
	(4)	B42874119C		D.	5,	3,	1,	2,	4
	(5)	E42817749G							
8.	(1)	M57906455S		A.	4,	1,	5,	3,	2
	(2)	N87077758S		B.	3,	4,	1,	5,	2
	(3)	N87707757B		C.	4,	1,	5,	2,	3
	(4)	M57877759B		D.	1,	5,	3,	2,	4
	(5)	M57906555S							
9.	(1)	C69336894Y		A.	2,	5,	3,	1,	4
	(2)	C69336684V		B.	3,	2,	5,	1,	4
	(3)	C69366887W		C.	3,	1,	4,	5,	2
	(4)	C69366994Y		D.	2,	5,	1,	3,	4
	(5)	C69336865V							
10.	(1)	A56247181D		A.	1,	5,	3,	2,	4
	(2)	A56272128P		B.	3,	1,	5,	2,	4
	(3)	H56247128D		C.	3,	2,	1,	5,	4
	(4)	H56272288P		D.	1,	5,	2,	3,	4
	(5)	A56247188D							

KEY (CORRECT ANSWERS)

1. D 6. D
2. B 7. B
3. A 8. A
4. C 9. A
5. C 10. D

TEST 10

DIRECTIONS: Answer the following questions on the basis of the instructions, the code, and the sample questions given below. Assume that an officer at a certain location is equipped with a two-way radio to keep him in constant touch with his security headquarters. Radio messages and replies are given in code form, as follows:

CODE TABLE

Radio Code for Situation	J	P	M	F	B
Radio Code for Action to be Taken	o	r	a	z	q
Radio Response for Action Being Taken	1	2	3	4	5

Assume that each of the above capital letters is the radio code for a particular type of situation, that the small letter below each capital letter is the radio code for the action an officer is directed to take, and that the number directly below each small letter is the radio response an officer should make to indicate what action was actually taken.

In each of the following questions, the code letter for the action directed (Column 2) and the code number for the action taken (Column 3) should correspond to the capital letters in Column 1.

INSTRUCTIONS: If only Column 2 is different from Column 1, mark your answer I.
If only Column 3 is different from Column 1, mark your answer II.
If both Column 2 and Column 3 are different from Column I, mark your answer III.
If both Columns 2 and 3 are the same as Column 1, mark your answer IV.

SAMPLE QUESTION

Column 1	Column 2	Column 3
JPFMB	orzaq	12453

The CORRECT answer is: A. I B. II C. III D. IV

The code letters in Column 2 are correct, but the numbers "53" in Column 3 should be "35." Therefore, the answer is B. Now answe the following questions according to the above rules.

	Column 1	Column 2	Column 3	
1.	PBFJM	rqzoa	25413	1.____
2.	MPFBJ	zrqao	32541	2.____
3.	JBFPM	oqzra	15432	3.____
4.	BJPMF	qaroz	51234	4.____
5.	PJFMB	rozaq	21435	5.____
6.	FJBMP	zoqra	41532	6.____

KEY (CORRECT ANSWERS)

1. D
2. C
3. B
4. A
5. D
6. A

NUMBER AND LETTER SERIES

COMMENTARY

One of the most searching types of the arithmetic reasoning question—a basic staple of tests of general and mental ability—is the number-series problem, in which a series of single numbers (or paired numbers) is presented, which follow a certain rule or sequence. The examinee is to select the next number (or pair of numbers) if the series were to be continued in this manner.

More difficult still, and on the highest level of difficulty is the letter-series question, wherein a series of letters, instead of numbers, is to be followed according to a definite order. Here, the element of abstractness serves to add further complexity to the problem.

Suggestion: In solving alphabetic series and progressions, it is wise to write out the alphabet and keep it in front of you. With this visual and aid immediately available, the key to each series can then be solved much more easily that way.

The questions in this section test your ability to see relationships between the elements of a series. These questions are sometimes referred to as series or progressions, and, in them, the candidate is asked to determine the rule that binds the elements together and then select the following element(s) according to that rule.

NUMBER SERIES/ONE NUMBER

SAMPLE QUESTIONS

DIRECTIONS: Each of the three sample questions presents a series of six numbers. Each series of numbers is made up according to a certain rule or order. You are to find what the next number in the series should be if the series were to be continued in this sequence.

1. 2 4 6 8 10 12
   - A. 14
   - B. 16
   - C. 18
   - D. 20
   - E. None of the above

1.____

Explanation: In Question 1, the rule is to add 2 to each number (2+2 = 4; 4 + 2 = 6, etc.). The net number in the series is 14 (12+2 = 14). Since 14 is lettered A among the suggested answers, A is the correct answer.

2. 7 8 6 7 5 6
   - A. 2
   - B. 3
   - C. 4
   - D. 5
   - E. None of the above

2.____

Explanation: In Question 2, the rule is to add 1 to the first number, subtract 2 from the next, add 1, subtract 2, and so on. The next number in the series is 4; letter C is the correct answer.

3. 3 6 9 12 15 18

3.____

Explanation: In Question 3, the rule is to add 3, making 21 the next number in the series. The correct answer to Question 3 is *none of the above*, since 39, 40, 45, and 59 are all incorrect answers; therefore, E is the correct answer.

NUMBER SERIES/ONE NUMBER
EXAMINATION SECTION
TEST 1

DIRECTIONS: Each of the following questions presents a series of single numbers. Five possible answers are given. From these choices, you are to find what the next number in the series should be if the series were to be continued in this sequence. *PRINT THE LETTER OF THE CORRECT ANSWER IN THE SPACE AT THE RIGHT.*

1. 3 13 4 15 5 7 6 19 7
   A. 20   B. 23   C. 21   D. 25   D. 27   1.____

2. 20 25 23 28 26 31 29 34
   A. 33   B. 32   C. 31   D. 30   E. 34   2.____

3. 9 24 39 54 69 84 99 114
   A. 129   B. 124   C. 128   D. 130   E. 126   3.____

4. 20 29 37 44 50 55 59
   A. 61   B. 62   C. 63   D. 64   E. 66   4.____

5. 20 21 23 26 30 35 41 48
   A. 55   B. 56   C. 54   D. 59   E. 57   5.____

6. 8 10 14 20 28 38 50 64
   A. 80   B. 72   C. 71   D. 73   E. 75   6.____

7. 6 7 9 12 16 21 28 35
   A. 40   B. 47   C. 50   D. 45   E. 43   7.____

8. 8 11 16 24 34 47
   A. 61   B. 62   C. 55   D. 60   E. 63   8.____

9. 3 8 14 25 37 54
   A. 67   B. 69   C. 68   D. 70   E. 72   9.____

10. 5 15 23 29 39 47 53 63
   A. 71   B. 72   C. 69   D. 73   E. 70   10.____

KEY (CORRECT ANSWERS)

1.	C	6.	A
2.	B	7.	E
3.	A	8.	B
4.	B	9.	E
5.	B	10.	A

TEST 2

DIRECTIONS: Each of the following questions presents a series of single numbers. Five possible answers are given. From these choices, you are to find what the next number in the series should be if the series were to be continued in this sequence. *PRINT THE LETTER OF THE CORRECT ANSWER IN THE SPACE AT THE RIGHT.*

1. 2 4 8 16 32 64 128
   A. 228   B. 130   C. 248   D. 264   E. 256

   1.____

2. 4 8 16 24 32 40 48
   A. 64   B. 56   C. 96   D. 62   E. 84

   2.____

3. 2 4 4 8 8 16 16
   A. 54   B. 48   C. 16   D. 32   E. 36

   3.____

4. 3 6 18 36 108 216 648
   A. 1946   B. 1944   C. 1296   D. 1056   E. 1488

   4.____

5. 10 13 11 14 12 15 13
   A. 14   B. 11   C. 15   D. 17   E. 16

   5.____

6. 2 6 18 54 162 486
   A. 1556   B. 496   C. 1286   D. 1458   E. 1552

   6.____

7. 4 20 35 49 62 74
   A. 82   B. 85   C. 93   D. 94   E. 96

   7.____

8. 10 15 12 17 14 19
   A. 22   B. 24   C. 21   D. 14   E. 16

   8.____

9. 4 10 8 14 12 18
   A. 16   B. 20   C. 24   D. 22   E. 21

   9.____

10. 10 18 15 23 20 28
    A. 23   B. 24   C. 25   D. 36   E. 40

    10.____

KEY (CORRECT ANSWERS)

1. E   6. D
2. B   7. B
3. D   8. E
4. C   9. A
5. E   10. C

TEST 3

NUMBER SERIES/TWO NUMBERS

SAMPLE QUESTIONS

DIRECTIONS: These questions are more difficult. In these, the arrangement is more complicated, and the answer is chosen from groups of two numbers, of which one group gives the next two numbers in the series

1. 1 1 2 1 3 1 4
   A. 1 5   B. 4 1   C. 5 1   D. 5 5   E. 6 1

   1.____

Explanation: The series consists of 1's alternating with numbers in ascending numerical order. The next two numbers would be 5 and 1. Therefore, C is the correct answer.

2. 2 8 3 7 5 6 8 5
   A. 10 6   B. 11 3   C. 11 4   D. 12 4   E. 12 6

   2.____

Explanation: This series consists of a sub-series for which the rule is to add 1, add 2, add 3, and add 4, alternating with another series in descending numerical order. The next number in the first sub-series would be 8 + 4, or 12; and the next number in the descending series would be 4. Therefore, D is the correct answer.

DIRECTIONS: Each of the following questions presents a series of single numbers. Five possible answers are given. From these choices, you are to find what the next number in the series should be if the series were to be continued in this sequence. *PRINT THE LETTER OF THE CORRECT ANSWER IN THE SPACE AT THE RIGHT.*

1. 3 4 3 5 3 6 3 7 3
   A. 8 3   B. 9 3   C. 9 4   D. 4 8   E. 7 5

   1.____

2. 50 2 48 4 6 6 44
   A. 8 46   B. 8 42   C. 4 28   D. 4 48   E. 8 44

   2.____

3. 40 39 43 38 6 37 49 36
   A. 37 51   B. 39 52   C. 51 37   D. 35 52   E. 52 35

   3.____

4. 50 51 49 53 47 56 44 60 40
   A. 60 40   B. 35 60   C. 60 35   D. 65 35   E. 35 65

   4.____

5. 1 100 2 50 4 25 8
   A. 12.5 4   B. 12.5 16   C. 16 12.5   D. 8.25 16   E. 16 8.25

   5.____

6. 1 25 2 24 4 22 7 19 11
   A. 15 16   B. 16 16   C. 16 15   D. 18 17   E. 17 18

   6.____

7. 2 4 6 8 12 14 18 20
   A. 26 22   B. 26 24   C. 22 26   D. 21 24   E. 24 26

   7.____

107

2 (#3)

8. 1 2 4 8 16 32
   A. 48 64   B. 64 128   C. 64 72   D. 63 129   E. 72 64

9. 10 50 13 54 16 58 19 62
   A. 22 66   B. 66 22   C. 64 20   D. 66 20   E. 20 66

10. 2 60 12 58 22 56 32
    A. 36 46   B. 42 54   C. 56 42   D. 42 56   E. 54 42

11. 2 90 4 80 6 70 8 60
    A. 12 52   B. 50 10   C. 10 50   D. 12 50   E. 50 12

12. 10 70 11 67 13 64 16 61
    A. 19 58   B. 20 58   C. 18 58   D. 58 20   E. 58 19

13. 10 20 30 12 23 26 14 26 22 16
    A. 19 29   B. 29 18   C. 29 19   D. 18 29   E. 30 18

14. 2 5 4 6 8 8 14 11 22 15
    A. 32 20   B. 30 20   C. 20 32   D. 31 21   E. 20 30

15. 10 15 20 11 17 23 12 19 26 13 21 29 14
    A. 16 29   B. 15 23   C. 23 32   D. 32 23   E. 23 15

8._____
9._____
10._____
11._____
12._____
13._____
14._____
15._____

KEY (CORRECT ANSWERS)

1.	A	6.	A	11.	C
2.	B	7.	E	12.	B
3.	E	8.	B	13.	B
4.	D	9.	A	14.	A
5.	B	10.	E	15.	C

TEST 4

DIRECTIONS: Each of the following questions presents a series of single numbers. Five possible answers are given. From these choices, you are to find what the next number in the series should be if the series were to be continued in this sequence. *PRINT THE LETTER OF THE CORRECT ANSWER IN THE SPACE AT THE RIGHT.*

1. 150 120 149 118 147 114 044 108 140
   A. 104 138   B. 102 136   C. 135 140   D. 100 135   E. 135 100

   1.____

2. 10 11 12 11 12 13 12 13 14 13 14 15 14
   A. 15 16   B. 13 14   C. 14 15   D. 16 15   E. 15 14

   2.____

3. 2 4 5 6 11 10 20 16 32 24
   A. 34 46   B. 32 46   C. 48 32   D. 46 32   E. 47 34

   3.____

4. 1 2 3 2 4 6 3 6 9 4 8 12 5
   A. 9 15   B. 9 14   C. 11 16   D. 10 14   E. 10 15

   4.____

5. 1 2 3 4 4 4 7 6 5 10 8 6
   A. 10 13   B. 13 10   C. 12 10   D. 12 9   E. 10 9

   5.____

6. 1 2 3 5 5 7 9 8 11 13 11
   A. 15 17   B. 17 15   C. 18 15   D. 15 18   E. 16 18

   6.____

7. 10 12 13 14 15 17 18 19 20 22
   A. 23 24   B. 24 23   C. 23 23   D. 22 24   E. 24 22

   7.____

8. 2 3 4 4 8 6 10 7 14 9 16 10 20 12
   A. 13 22   B. 12 24   C. 20 12   D. 24 12   E. 22 13

   8.____

9. 1 2 2 5 4 9 5 12 7 16 8 19 10 23
   A. 27 12   B. 12 27   C. 11 26   D. 26 11   E. 12 28

   9.____

10. 100 106 98 103 97 99 95 96 94 92 92 89 91 85
    A. 82 89   B. 89 82   C. 90 81   D. 81 90   E. 90 83

    10.____

KEY (CORRECT ANSWERS)

1. D   6. A
2. A   7. A
3. E   8. E
4. E   9. C
5. B   10. B

TEST 5

LETTER SERIES

SAMPLE QUESTIONS

DIRECTIONS: In each of these questions, there is a series of letters which follow some definite order, and underneath there are five sets of two letters each. Look at the letters in the series and determine what the order is; then, from the suggested answers below, select the set that gives the next two letters in the series in their correct order.

1. X C X D X E X
    A. F X   B. F G   C. X F   D. E F   E. X G

1._____

Explanation: The series consists of X's alternating with letters in alphabetical order. The next two letters would be F and X; therefore, A is the correct answer.

2. A B D C E F H
    A. G H   B. I G   C. G I   D. K L   E. I H

2._____

Explanation: If you compare this series with the alphabet, you will find that it goes along in pairs, the first pair in their usual order and the next pair in reverse order. The last letter given in the series is the second letter of the pair G-H, which is in reverse order. The first missing letter must, therefore, be G. The next pair of letters would be I-J, in that order; the second of the missing letters is I. The alternative you look for, then, is G I, which is lettered C.

DIRECTIONS: Each of the following questions presents a series of single letters. Five possible answers are given. From these choices, find what the next letter in the series should be if the series were to continue in this sequence. *PRINT THE LETTER OF THE CORRECT ANSWER IN THE SPACE AT THE RIGHT.*

1. B A C A D A E A F A G A
    A. H A   B. A H   C. K A   D. L A   E. A K

1._____

2. A B D C B D D B D E B D F B D G B
    A. H D   B. B G   C. D B   D. D H   E. D J

2._____

3. J I H G F E D C
    A. BC   B. CB   C. BA   D. AB   E. DC

3._____

4. Z Y X W V U T S R
    A. PQ   B. PO   C. OP   D. NP   E. QP

4._____

5. X W V X U X T X S X R
    A. X O   B. Q X   C. X P   D. P X   E. X Q

5._____

6. K L N M O P Q S T
    A. V U   B. U V   C. W V   D. V W   E. W U

6._____

7. A B C F E D G H I L K J M
    A. O N   B. N O   C. O M   D. M O   E. M N

7._____

110

2 (#5)

8. Z Y W X V U S T R Q O P N M
   A. K J   B. J K   C. K L   D. L K   E. L M   8.____

9. Y Z X W U V T S Q R P O M N
   A. K J   B. L K   C. K L   D. J K   E. M L   9.____

10. Z Y X U V W T S R O P Q N M L
    A. I K   B. K I   C. I J   D. K J   E. J I   10.____

11. A C E G I K M O Q
    A. S U   B. S T   C. R S   D. R T   E. U S   11.____

12. Z U X V T R P N L
    A. K L   B. K J   C. H J   D. L K   E. J H   12.____

13. Z W T Q N K H
    A. E B   B. E C   D. F B   D. F C   E. C F   13.____

14. A D G J M P S
    A. V W   B. U W   C. U V   D. V Y   E. W U   14.____

15. A D F I K N P S
    A. W U   B. U W   C. U X   D. U V   E. V U   15.____

KEY (CORRECT ANSWERS)

1.	A	6.	A	11.	A
2.	D	7.	B	12.	E
3.	C	8.	C	13.	A
4.	E	9.	B	14.	D
5.	E	10.	E	15.	C

TEST 6

DIRECTIONS: Each of the following questions presents a series of single letters. Five possible answers are given. From these choices, you are to find what the next letter in the series should be if the series were to be continued in this sequence. *PRINT THE LETTER OF THE CORRECT ANSWER IN THE SPACE AT THE RIGHT.*

1. A C E D G I H K M L
   A. O P   B. O Q   C. Q P   D. P Q   E. Q O   1.____

2. Z X V W T R S P N O
   A. J K   B. K J   C. L K   D. K L   E. K I   2.____

3. B A D C F E H G J I L
   A. K N   B. K M   C. N K   D. L K   E. K L   3.____

4. Y Z W X U V S T Q R O P M
   A. L K   B. K L   C. N L   D. N K   E. L N   4.____

5. A B D C E F H G I J L K M N
   A. R P   B. P O   C. O P   D. P Q   E. Q P   5.____

6. A B C D F E G H I J L K M
   A. O N   B. N O   C. P O   D. O P   E. M N   6.____

7. Z Y X U V W T S R
   A. O P   B. P O   C. O N   D. N O   E. P Q   7.____

8. A B C B C D C D E D E F E
   A. G H   B. G F   C. E F   D. F G   E. F E   8.____

9. X V T R P F H J
   A. K L   B. L M   C. K M   D. M N   E. L N   9.____

10. C C F F I I L L V V S S P P M M
    A. K K   B. I I   C. J J   D. H H   E. G G   10.____

11. A N C O E P G
    A. H I   B. R H   C. R I   D. Q I   E. I Q   11.____

12. B D F H J L N
    A. P Q   B. S Q   C. R P   D. P R   E. Q S   12.____

13. Z X V T R P N
    A. J L   B. M L   C. L K   D. M K   E. L J   13.____

14. A B D G K
    A. L O   B. O Q   C. Q O   D. P L   E. P W   14.____

112

15. F H K O T R O   15.____
    A. J G   B. L F   C. K G   D. J F   E. K F

KEY (CORRECT ANSWERS)

1.	B	6.	B	11.	D
2.	E	7.	A	12.	D
3.	A	8.	D	13.	E
4.	D	9.	E	14.	E
5.	B	10.	C	15.	E

TEST 7

DIRECTIONS: Each of the following questions presents a series of single letters. Five possible answers are given. From these choices, you are to find what the next letter in the series should be if the series were to be continued in this sequence. *PRINT THE LETTER OF THE CORRECT ANSWER IN THE SPACE AT THE RIGHT.*

1. B B G G L L O O R R S S
   A. U U   B. V V   C. T T   D. W W   E. X X

   1.____

2. A C B D C E D F E G
   A. F G   B. G H   C. H F   D. F H   E. G F

   2.____

3. D H F J H L J N
   A. M N   B. L N   C. L O   D. L P   E. P N

   3.____

4. A C E F H J K M O
   A. M O Q   B. R T P   C. N Q O   D. P T R   E. P R T

   4.____

5. B G L Q V E J O
   A. P U   B. T Y   C. R W   D. S X   E. Y Z

   5.____

6. A F G B G H C H I D
   A. F K   B. G L   C. H M   D. I N   E. I J

   6.____

7. A K B L C M D N
   A. E M   B. F N   C. J L   D. E J   E. E O

   7.____

8. P R K M F H
   A. C E   B. A C   C. D F   D. B D   E. C E

   8.____

9. A G M S Y B H N
   A. P V   B. Q W   C. R X   D. S Y   E. T Z

   9.____

10. B E C F D G Y V X U
    A. W T   B. W V   C. V U   D. T S   E. U T

    10.____

KEY (CORRECT ANSWERS)

1. C   6. E
2. D   7. E
3. D   8. B
4. E   9. E
5. B   10. A

BASIC FUNDAMENTALS OF FILING SCIENCE

TABLE OF CONTENTS

	Page
I. COMMENTARY	1
II. BASICS OF FILING	1
1. Types of Files	1
a. Shannon File	1
b. Spindle File	1
c. Box File	1
d. Flat File	1
e. Bellows File	1
f. Vertical File	1
g. Clip File	1
h. Visible File	2
i. Rotary File	2
2. Aids in Filing	2
3. Variations of Filing Systems	2
4. Centralized Filing	2
5. Methods of Filing	3
a. Alphabetic Filing	3
b. Subject Filing	3
c. Geographical Filing	3
d. Chronological Filing	3
e. Numerical Filing	3
6. Indexing	3
7. Alphabetizing	4
III. RULES FOR INDEXING AND ALPHABETIZING	4
IV. OFFICIAL EXAMINATION DIRECTIONS AND RULES	8
1. Official Directions	8
2. Official Rules For Alphabetical Filing	9
a. Names of Individuals	9
b. Names of Business Organizations	9
3. Sample Question	9

BASIC FUNDAMENTALS OF FILING SCIENCE

I. COMMENTARY

Filing is the systematic arrangement and storage of papers, cards, forms, catalogues, etc. so that they may be found easily and quickly. The importance of an efficient filing system cannot be emphasized too strongly. The filed materials form records which may be needed quickly to settle questions that may cause embarrassing situations if such evidence is not available. In addition to keeping papers in order so that they are readily available, the filing system must also be designed to keep papers in good condition. A filing system must be planned so that papers may be filed easily, withdrawn easily, and as quickly returned to their proper place. The cost of a filing system is also an important factor

The need for a filing system arose when the businessman began to carry on negotiations on a large scale. He could no longer be intimate with the details of his business. What was needed in the early era was a spindle or pigeon-hole desk. Filing in pigeon-hole desks is now almost completely extinct. It was an unsatisfactory practice since pigeon holes were not labeled, and the desk was an untidy mess.

II. BASIS OF FILING

The science of filing is an exact one and entails a thorough understanding of basic facts, materials, and methods. An overview of this important information now follows.

1. Types of Files

    a. Shannon File: This consists of a board, at one end of which are fastened two arches which may be opened laterally.

    b. Spindle File: This consists of a metal or wood base to which is attached a long, pointed spike. Papers are pushed down on the spike as received. This file is useful for temporary retention of papers.

    c. Box File: This is a heavy cardboard or metal box, opening from the side like a book.

    d. Flat File: This consists of a series of shallow drawers or trays, arranged like drawers in a cabinet.

    e. Bellows File: This is a heavy cardboard container with alphabetized or compartment sections, the ends of which are enclosed in such a manner that they resemble an accordion.

    f. Vertical File: This consists of one or more drawers in which the papers are stood on edge, usually in folders, and are indexed by guides. A series of two or more drawers in one unit is the usual file cabinet.

    g. Clip File: This file has a large clip attached to a board and is very similar to the Shannon File.

h. Visible File: Cards are filed flat in an overlapping arrangement which leaves a part of each card visible at all times.

i. Rotary File: The rotary file has a number of visible card files attached to a post around which they can be revolved. The wheel file has visible cards which rotate around a horizontal axis.

j. Tickler File: This consists of cards or folders marked with the days of the month, in which materials are filed and turned up on the appropriate day of the month.

2. Aids in Filing

   a. Guides: Guides are heavy cardboard, pasteboard, or Bristol-board sheets the same size as folders. At the top is a tab on which is marked or printed the distinguishing letter, words, or numbers indicating the material filed in a section of the drawer.

   b. Sorting Trays: Sorting trays are equipped with alphabetical guides to facilitate the sorting of papers preparatory to placing them in a file.

   c. Coding: Once the classification or indexing caption has been determined, it must be indicated on the letter for filing purposes.

   d. Cross-Reference: Some letters or papers might easily be called for under two or more captions. For this purpose, a cross-reference card or sheet is placed in the folder or in the index.

3. Variations of Filing Systems

   a. Variadex Alphabetic Index: Provides for more effective expansion of the alphabetic system.

   b. Triple-Check Numeric Filing: Entails a multiple cross-reference, as the name implies.

   c. Variadex Filing: Makes use of color as an aid in filing.

   d. Dewey Decimal System: The system is a numeric one used in libraries or for filing library materials in an office. This special type of filing system is used where material is grouped in finely divided categories, such as in libraries. With this method, all material to be filed is divided into ten major groups, from 000 to 900, and then subdivided into tens, units, and decimals.

4. Centralized Filing

Centralized filing means keeping the files in one specific or central location. Decentralized filing means putting away papers in files of individual departments. The first step in the organization of a central filing department is to make a careful canvass of all desks in the offices. In this manner we can determine just what material needs to be filed, and what information each desk occupant requires from the central file. Only papers which may be used at some time by persons in the various offices should be placed in the central file. A paper that is to be used at some time by persons in the various offices should be placed in the central file. A paper that is to be used by one department only should never be filed in the central file.

5. Methods of Filing

   While there are various methods used for filing, actually there are only five basic systems: alphabetical, subject, numerical, geographic, and chronological. All other systems are derived from one of these or from a combination of two or more of them. Since the purpose of a filing system is to store business records systemically so that any particular record can be found almost instantly when required, filing requires, in addition to the proper kinds of equipment and supplies, an effective method of indexing.
   There are five basic systems of filing:

   a. Alphabetic Filing: Most filing is alphabetical. Other methods, as described below, require extensive alphabetization. In alphabetical filing, lettered dividers or guides are arranged in alphabetic sequence. Material to be filed is placed behind the proper guide. All materials under each letter are also arranged alphabetically. Folders are used unless the file is a card index.

   b. Subject Filing: This method is used when a single, complete file on a certain subject is desired. A subject file is often maintained to assemble all correspondence on a certain subject. Such files are valuable in connection with insurance claims, contract negotiations, personnel, and other investigations, special programs, and similar subjects.

   c. Geographical File: Materials are filed according to location: states, cities, counties, or other subdivisions. Statistics and tax information are often filed in this manner.

   d. Chronological File: Records are filed according to date. This method is used especially in "tickler" files that have guides numbered 1 to 31 for each day of the month. Each number indicates the day of the month when the filed item requires attention.

   e. Numerical File: This method requires an alphabetic card index giving name and number. The card index is used to locate records numbered consecutively in the files according to date received or sequence in which issued, such as licenses, permits, etc.

6. Indexing

   Determining the name or title under which an item is to be filed is known as indexing. For example, how would a letter from Robert E. Smith be filed? The name would be rearranged Smith, Robert E., so that the letter would be filed under the last name.

7. Alphabetizing

The arranging of names for filing is known as alphabetizing. For example, suppose you have four letters indexed under the names Johnson, Becker, Roe, and Stern. How should these letters be arranged in the files so that they may be found easily? You would arrange the four names alphabetically, thus Becker, Johnson, Roe, and Stern.

III. RULES FOR INDEXING AND ALPHABETIZING

1. The names of persons are to be transposed. Write the surname first, then the given name, and, finally, the middle name or initial. Then arrange the various names according to the alphabetic order of letters throughout the entire name. If there is a title, consider that after the middle name or initial.

NAMES	INDEXED AS
Arthur L. Bright	Bright, Arthur L.
Arthur S. Bright	Bright, Arthur S.
P.E. Cole	Cole, P.E.
Dr. John C. Fox	Fox, John C. (Dr.)

2. If a surname includes the same letters of another surname, with one or more additional letters added to the end, the shorter surname is placed first regardless of the given name or the initial of the given name.

NAMES	INDEXED AS
Robert E. Brown	Brown, Robert E.
Gerald A. Browne	Browne, Gerald A.
William O. Brownell	Brownell, William O.

3. Firm names are alphabetized under the surnames. Words like the, an, a, of, and for, are not considered.

NAMES	INDEXED AS
Bank of America	Bank of America
Bank Discount Dept.	Bank Discount Dept.
The Cranford Press	Cranford Press, The
Nelson Dwyer & Co.	Dwyer, Nelson, & Co.
Sears, Roebuck & Co.	Sears Roebuck & Co.
Montgomery Ward & Co.	Ward, Montgomery, & Co.

4. The order of filing is determined first of all by the first letter of the names to be filed. If the first letters are the same, the order is determined by the second letters, and so on. In the following pairs of names, the order is determined by the letters underlined:

    | <u>A</u>usten | Ha<u>y</u>es | Ha<u>n</u>son | Har<u>v</u>ey | Hea<u>th</u> | Gree<u>n</u> | Schwa<u>rt</u>z |
    | <u>B</u>aker | H<u>e</u>ath | Har<u>p</u>er | Har<u>w</u>ood | Hea<u>to</u>n | Gree<u>ne</u> | Schwa<u>r</u>z |

5. When surnames are alike, those with initials only precede those with given names, unless the first initial comes alphabetically after the first letter of the name.

    Gleason, S.   *but,* Abbott, Mary
    Gleason, S.W.   Abbott, W.B.
    Gleason, Sidney

120

6. Hyphenated names are treated as if spelled without the hyphen.
   - Lloyd, Paul N.
   - Lloyd, Robert
   - Lloyd-Jones, James
   - Lloyd-Thomas, A.S.

7. Company names composed of single letters which are not used as abbreviations precede the other names beginning with the same letter.
   - B & S Garage
   - E Z Duplicator Co.
   - B X Cable Co.
   - Eagle Typewriter Co.
   - Babbitt, R.N.
   - Edison Company

8. The ampersand (&) and the apostrophe (') in firm names are disregarded in alphabetizing.
   - Nelson & Niller
   - M & C Amusement Corp.
   - Nelson, Walter J.
   - M C Art Assn.
   - Nelson's Bakery

9. Names beginning with Mac, Mc, or M' are usually placed in regular order as spelled. Some filing systems file separately names beginning with Mc.
   - MacDonald, R.J.
   - Mazza, Anthony
   - MacDonald, S.B.
   - McAdam, Wm.
   - Mace, Wm.
   - McAndrews, Jerry

10. Names beginning with St. are listed as if the name Saint were spelled in full. Numbered street names and all abbreviated names are treated as if spelled out in full.
    - Saginaw
    - Fifth Avenue Hotel
    - Hart Mfg. Co.
    - St. Louis
    - 42nd Street Dress Shop
    - Hart, Martin
    - St. Peter's Rectory
    - Hart, Chas.
    - Hart, Thos.
    - Sandford
    - Hart, Charlotte
    - Hart, Thomas A.
    - Smith, Wm.
    - Hart, Jas.
    - Hart, Thos. R.
    - Smith, Willis
    - Hart, Janice

11. Federal, state, or city departments of government should be placed alphabetically under the governmental branch controlling them.
    - Illinois, State of – Departments and Commissions
      - Banking Dept.
      - Employment Bureau
    - United States Government Departments
      - Commerce
      - Defense
      - State
      - Treasury

12. Alphabetic Order: Each word in a name is an indexing unit. Arrange the names in alphabetic order by comparing similar units in each name. Consider the second units only when the first units are identical. Consider the third units only when both the first and second units are identical.

13. Single Surnames or Initials: A surname, when used alone, precedes the same surname with a first name or initial. A surname with a first initial only precedes a surname with a complete first name. This rule is sometimes stated, "nothing comes before something."

14. Surname Prefixes: A surname prefix is not a separate indexing unit, but it is considered part of the surname. These prefixes include: d', D', Da, de, De, Del, Des, Di, Du, Fitz., La, Le, Mc, Mac, 'c, O', St., Van, Van der, Von, Von der, and others. The prefixes M', Mac, and Mc are indexed and filed exactly as they are spelled.

15. Names of Firms: Names of firms and institutions are indexed and filed exactly as they are written when they do not contain the complete name of an individual.

16. Names of Firms Containing Complete Individual Names: When the firm or institution name includes the complete name of an individual, the units are transposed for indexing in the same way as the name of an individual.

17. Article "The": When the article "the" occurs at the beginning of a name, it is placed at the end in parentheses but it is not moved. In both cases, it is not an indexing unit and is disregarded in filing.

18. Hyphenated Names: Hyphenated firm names are considered as separate indexing units. Hyphenated surnames of individuals are considered as one indexing unit; this applies also to hyphenated names of individuals whose complete names are part of a firm name.

19. Abbreviations: Abbreviations are considered as though the name were written in full; however, single letters other than abbreviations are considered as separate indexing units.

20. Conjunctions, Prepositions, and Firm Endings: Conjunctions and prepositions, such as and, for, in, of, are disregarded in indexing and filing but are not omitted or their order changed when writing names on cards and folders. Firm endings, such as Ltd., Inc., So., Son, Bros., Mfg., and Corp., are treated as a unit in indexing and filing and are considered as though spelled in full, such as Brothers and Incorporated.

21. One of Two Words: Names that may be spelled either as one or two words are indexed and filed as one word.

22. Compound Geographic Names: Compound geographic names are considered as separate indexing and filing units, except when the first part of the name is not an English word, such as the Los in Los Angeles.

23. Titles or degrees of individuals, whether preceding or following the name, are not considered in indexing or filing. They are placed in parentheses after the given name or initial. Terms that designate seniority, such as Jr., Sr., 2d, are also placed in parentheses and are considered for indexing and filing only when the names to be indexed are otherwise identical.

Exception A: When the name of an individual consists of a title and one name only, such as Queen Elizabeth, it is not transposed and the title is considered for indexing and filing.

Exception B: When a title or foreign article is the initial word of a firm or association name, it is considered for indexing and filing.

24. Possessives: When a word ends in apostrophe s, the s is not considered in indexing and filing. However, when a word ends in s apostrophe, because the s is part of the original word, it is considered. This rule is sometimes stated, "Consider everything up to the apostrophe."

25. United States and Foreign Government Names: Names pertaining to the federal government are indexed and filed under United States Government and then subdivided by title of the department, bureau, division, commission, or board. Names pertaining to foreign governments are indexed and filed under names of countries and then subdivided by title of the department, bureau, division, commission, or board. Phrases, such as department of, bureau of, division of, commission of, board of, when used in titles of governmental bodies, are placed in parentheses after the word they modify, but are disregarded in indexing and filing. Such phrases, however, are considered in indexing and filing governmental names.

26. Other Political Subdivisions: Names pertaining to other political subdivisions, such as states, counties, cities, or towns, are indexed and filed under the name of the political subdivision and then subdivided by the title of the department, bureau, division, commission, or board.

27. When the same name appears with different addresses, the names are indexed as usual and arranged alphabetically according to city or town. The State is considered only when there is duplication of both individual or company name and city name. If the same name is located at different addresses within the same city, then the names are arranged alphabetically by streets. If the same name is located at more than one address on the same street then the names are arranged from the lower to the higher street number.

28. Numbers: Any number in a name is considered as though it were written in words, and it is indexed and filed as one unit.

29. Bank Names: Because the names of many banking institutions are alike in several respects, as First National Bank, Second National Bank, etc., banks are indexed and filed first by city location, then by bank name, with the state location written in parentheses and considered only if necessary.

30. Married Women: The legal name of a married woman is the one used for filing purposes. Legally, a man's surname is the only part of a man's name a woman assumes when she marries. Her legal name, therefore, could be either:
    a. Her own first and middle names together with her husband's surname, or
    b. Her own first name and maiden surname, together with her husband's surname.

Mrs. is placed in parentheses at the end of the name. Her husband's first and middle names are given in parentheses below her legal name.

31. An alphabetically arranged list of names illustrating many difficult points of alphabetizing follows:

COLUMN I	COLUMN II
Abbot, W.B.	54th St. Tailor Shop
Abbot, Alice	Forstall, W.J.
Allen Alexander B.	44th St. Garage
Allen, Alexander B., Inc.	M A Delivery Co.
Andersen, Hans	M & C Amusement Corp.
Andersen, Hans E.	M C Art Assn.
Andersen, Hans E., Jr.	MacAdam, Wm.
Anderson, Andrew Andrews,	Macaulay, James
George Brown Motor Co., Boston	MacAulay, Wilson
Brown Motor Co., Chicago	MacDonald, R.J.
Brown Motor Co., Philadelphia	Macdonald, S. B.
Brown Motor Co., San Francisco	Mace, Wm.
Dean, Anna	Mazza, Anthony
Dean, Anna F.	McAdam, Wm.
Dean, Anna Frances	McAndrews, Jerry
Dean & Co.	Meade & Clark Co.
Deane-Arnold Apartments	Meade, S.T.
Deane's Pharmacy	Meade, Soloman
Deans, Felix A.	Sackett Publishing Co.
Dean's Studio	Sacks, Robert
Deans, Wm.	St. Andrew Hotel
Deans & Williams	St. John, Homer W.
East Randolph	Saks, Isaac B.
East St. Louis	Stephens, Ira
Easton, Pa.	Stevens, Delevan
Eastport, Me.	Stevens, Delila

IV. OFFICIAL EXAMINATION DIRECTIONS AND RULES

To preclude the possibility of conflicting or varying methods of filing, explicit directions and express rules are given to the candidate before he answers the filing questions on an examination.
The most recent official directions and rules for the filing questions are given immediately hereafter.

OFFICIAL DIRECTIONS

Each of questions…to…consists of four (five) names. For each question, select the one of the four(five) names that should be first (second)(third)(last) if the four (five(names were arranged in alphabetical order in accordance with the rules for alphabetical filing given below. Read these rules carefully. Then, for each question, indicate in the correspondingly numbered row on the answer sheet the letter preceding the name that should be first(second)(third)(last) in alphabetical order.

OFFICIAL RULES FOR ALPHABETICAL FILING

Names of Individuals

1. The names of individuals are filed in strict alphabetical order, first according to the last name, then according to first name or initial, and, finally, according to middle name or initial. For example: William Jones precedes George Kirk and Arthur S. Blake precedes Charles M. Blake.
2. When the last names are identical, the one with an initial instead of a first name precedes the one "with a first name beginning with the same initial." For example: J. Green precedes Joseph Green.
3. When identical last names also have identical first names, the one without a middle name or initial precedes the one with a middle name or initial. For example: Robert Jackson precedes both Robert C. Jackson and Robert Chester Jackson.
4. When last names are identical and the first names are also identical, the one with a middle initial precedes the one with a middle name beginning with the same initial. For example: Peter A. Brown precedes Peter Alvin Brown.
5. Prefixes such as De, El, La, and Van are considered parts of the names they precede. For example: Wilfred DeWald precedes Alexander Duval.
6. Last names beginning with "Mac" or "Mc" are filed as spelled.
7. Abbreviated names are treated as if they were spelled out. For example: Jos. is filed as Joseph and Robt. is filed as Robert.
8. Titles and designations such as Dr., Mrs., Prof. are disregarding in filing.

Names of Business Organizations

1. The names of business organizations are filed exactly as written, except that an organization bearing the name of an individual is filed alphabetically according to the name of the individual in accordance with the rules for filing names of individuals given above. For example: Thomas Allison Machine Company precedes Northern Baking Company.
2. When numerals occur in a name, they are treated as if they were spelled out. For example: 6 stands for six and 4th stands for fourth.
3. When the following words occur in names, they are disregarded: the, of

SAMPLE QUESTION

Choose the name that should be filed third.
A. Fred Town (2)   B. Jack Towne (3)   C. D. Town (1)   D. Jack Stone (4)
The numbers in parentheses indicate the proper alphabetical order in which these names should be filed. Since the name that should be filed third is Jack Towne, the answer is (B).

FILING
EXAMINATION SECTION
TEST 1

DIRECTIONS: Each of the following questions contains four names. For each question, choose the name that should be FIRST if the four names are to be arranged in alphabetical order in accordance with the Rules for Alphabetical Filing given before. Read these rules carefully. Then, for each question, indicate in the space at the right the letter before the name that should be FIRST in alphabetical order.

SAMPLE QUESTION
A. Jane Earl   (2)
B. James A. Earle (4)
C. James Earl   (1)
D. J. Earle   (3)

The numbers in parentheses show the proper alphabetical order in which these names should be filed. Since the name that should be filed FIRST is James Earl, the answer to the Sample Question is C.

1. A. Majorca Leather Goods B. Robert Maiorca and Sons 1.____
   C. Maintenance Management Corp. D. Majestic Carpet Mills

2. A. Municipal Telephone Service B. Municipal Reference Library 2.____
   C. Municipal Credit Union D. Municipal Broadcasting System

3. A. Robert B. Pierce B. R. Bruce Pierce 3.____
   C. Ronald Pierce D. Robert Bruce Pierce

4. A. Four Seasons Sports Club B. 14 Street Shopping Center 4.____
   C. Forty Thieves Restaurant D. 42nd St. Theaters

5. A. Franco Franceschini B. Amos Franchini 5.____
   C. Sandra Franceschia D. Lilie Franchinesca

KEY (CORRECT ANSWERS)

1. C
2. D
3. B
4. D
5. C

TEST 2

DIRECTIONS: Each of the following questions contains four names. For each question, choose the name that should be FIRST if the four names are to be arranged in alphabetical order in accordance with the Rules for Alphabetical Filing given before. Read these rules carefully. Then, for each question, indicate in the space at the right the letter before the name that should be FIRST in alphabetical order.

    SAMPLE QUESTION
    A. Jane Earl   (2)
    B. James A. Earle (4)
    C. James Earl   (1)
    D. J. Earle   (3)

The numbers in parentheses show the proper alphabetical order in which these names should be filed. Since the name that should be filed FIRST is James Earl, the answer to the Sample Question is C.

1. A. Alan Carson, M.D.   B. The Andrew Carlton Nursing Home   1.____
   C. Prof., Alfred P. Carlton   D. Mr. A. Peter Carlton

2. A. Chas. A. Denner   B. H. Jeffrey Dener   2.____
   C. Charles Denner   D. Harold Dener

3. A. James C. Maziola   B. Joseph A. Mazzola   3.____
   C. James Maziola   D. J. Alfred Mazzola

4. A. Bureau of Family Affairs   B. Office of the Comptroller   4.____
   C. Department of Gas & Electricity   D. Board of Estimate

5. A. Robert Alan Pearson   B. John Charles Pierson   5.____
   C. Robert Allen Pearson   D. John Chester Pierson

6. A. The Johnson Manufacturing Co.   B. C.J. Johnston   6.____
   C. Bernard Johnsen   D. Prof. Corey Johnstone

7. A. Ninteenth Century Book Shop   B. Ninth Federal Bank   7.____
   C. 19th Hole Coffee Shop   D. 92nd St. Station

8. A. George S. McNeely   B. Hugh J. Macintosh   8.____
   C. Mr. G. Stephen McNeally   D. Mr. H. James Macintosh

KEY (CORRECT ANSWERS)

1. D
2. B
3. C
4. B
5. A
6. C
7. A
8. D

TEST 3

DIRECTIONS: Each of the following questions contains four names. For each question, choose the name that should be LAST if the four names are to be arranged in alphabetical order in accordance with the Rules for Alphabetical Filing given before. Read these rules carefully. Then, for each question, indicate in the space at the right the letter before the name that should be LAST in alphabetical order.

SAMPLE QUESTION
A. Jane Earl (2)
B. James A. Earle (4)
C. James Earl (1)
D. J. Earle (3)

The numbers in parentheses show the proper alphabetical order in which these names should be filed. Since the name that should be filed LAST is James A. Earle, the answer to the Sample Question is B.

1. A. Steiner, Michael B. Steinblau, Dr. Walter 1.____
   C. Steinet, Gary D. Stein, Prof. Edward

2. A. The Paper Goods Warehouse B. T. Pane and Sons Inc. 2.____
   C. Paley, Wallace D. Painting Supplies Inc.

3. A. D'Angelo, F. B. De Nove, C. 3.____
   C. Daniels, Frank D. Dovarre, Carl

4. A. Berene, Arnold B. Berene, Arnold L. 4.____
   C. Beren, Arnold Lee D. Berene, A.

5. A. Kallinski, Liza B. Kalinsky, L. 5.____
   C. Kallinky, E. D. Kallinsky, Elizabeth

6. A. Morgenom, Salvatore B. Megan, J. 6.____
   C. J. Morgenthal Consultant Services D. Morgan, Janet

7. A. Ritter, G. B. Ritter, George 7.____
   B. Riter, George H. D. Ritter, G.H.

8. A. Wheeler, Adele N. B. Wieler, Ada 8.____
   C. Weiler, Adelaide D. Wheiler, Adele

9. A. Macan, Toby B. Maccini, T. 9.____
   C. MacAvoy, Thomas D. Mackel, Theodore

10. A. Loomus, Kenneth B. Lomis Paper Supplies 10.____
    C. Loo, N. D. Loomis Machine Repair Company

131

KEY (CORRECT ANSWERS)

1. C
2. A
3. D
4. B
5. D

6. C
7. B
8. B
9. D
10. A

TEST 4

DIRECTIONS: In the following questions there are five notations numbered 1 through 5 shown in Column I. Each notation is made up of a supplier's name, a contract number, and a date and is to be filed according to the following rules:

First: File in alphabetical order
Second: When two or more notations have the same supplier, file according to the contract number in numerical order beginning with the lowest number.
Third: When two or more notations have the same supplier and contract number, file according to the date beginning with the earliest date.

In Column II the numbers 1 through 5 are arranged in four ways to show different possible orders in which the merchandise information might be filed. Pick the answer (A, B, C, or D) in Column II in which the notations are arranged according to the above filing rules.

SAMPLE QUESTION

COLUMN I			COLUMN II
1. Cluney	(4865)	6/17/72	A. 2, 3, 4, 1, 5
2. Roster	(2466)	5/10/71	B. 2, 5, 1, 3, 4
3. Altool	(7114)	10/15/72	C. 3, 2, 1, 4, 5
4. Cluney	(5276)	12/18/71	D. 3, 5, 1, 4, 2
5. Cluney	(4865)	4/8/72	

The correct way to file the notations is:
3. Altool   (7114)   10/15/72
5. Cluney   (4865)   4/8/72
1. Cluney   (4865)   6/17/72
4. Cluney   (5276)   12/18/71
2. Roster   (2466)   5/10/71

The correct filing order is shown by the numbers in front of each name (3, 5, 1, 4, 2). The answer to the Sample Question is the letter in Column II in front of the numbers 3, 5, 1, 4, 2. This answer is D.

1.
COLUMN I			COLUMN II
1. Fenten	(38511)	1/4/73	A. 3, 5, 2, 1, 4
2. Meadowlane	(5020)	11/1/72	B. 4, 1, 2, 5, 3
3. Whitehall	(36142)	6/22/72	C. 4, 2, 5, 3, 1
4. Clinton	(4141)	5/26/71	D. 5, 4, 3, 1, 2
5. Mester	(8006)	4/20/71	

2.
COLUMN I			COLUMN II
1. Harvard	(2286)	2/19/70	A. 2, 4, 3, 1, 5
2. Parker	(1781)	4/12/71	B. 2, 1, 3, 4, 5
3. Lenson	(9044)	6/6/72	C. 4, 1, 3, 2, 5
4. Brothers	(38380)	10/11/72	D. 5, 2, 3, 1, 4
5. Parker	(41400)	12/20/70	

2 (#4)

		COLUMN I			COLUMN II	
3.	1.	Newtone	(3197)	8/22/70	A. 1, 4, 2, 5, 3	3.____
	2.	Merritt	(4071)	8/8/72	B. 4, 2, 1, 5, 3	
	3.	Writebest	(60666)	4/7/71	C. 4, 5, 2, 1, 3	
	4.	Maltons	(34380)	3/30/72	D. 5, 2, 4, 3, 1	
	5.	Merrit	(4071)	7/16/71		
4.	1.	Weinburt	(45514)	6/4/71	A. 4, 5, 2, 1, 3	4.____
	2.	Owntye	(35860)	10/3/71	B. 4, 2, 5, 3, 1	
	3.	Weinburt	(45514)	2/1/71	C. 4, 2, 5, 1, 3	
	4.	Fasttex	(7677)	11/10/71	D. 4, 5, 2, 3, 1	
	5.	Owntye	(4574)	7/17/71		
5.	1.	Premier	(1003)	7/29/70	A. 2, 1, 4, 3, 5	5.____
	2.	Phylson	(0031)	5/5/71	B. 3, 5, 4, 1, 2	
	3.	Lathen	(3328)	10/3/71	C. 4, 1, 2, 3, 5	
	4.	Harper	(8046)	8/18/72	D. 4, 3, 5, 2, 1	
	5.	Lathen	(3328)	12/1/72		
6.	1.	Repper	(46071)	10/14/72	A. 3, 2, 4, 5, 1	6.____
	2.	Destex	(77271)	8/27/72	B. 3, 4, 2, 5, 1	
	3.	Clawson	(30736)	7/28/71	C. 3, 4, 5, 2, 1	
	4.	Destex	(77271)	8/17/71	D. 3, 5, 4, 2, 1	
	5.	Destex	(77271)	4/14/71		

KEY (CORRECT ANSWERS)

1. B
2. C
3. C
4. A
5. D
6. C

TEST 5

DIRECTIONS: Each of the following questions represents five cards to be filed, numbered 1 through 5 shown in Column I. Each card is made up of the employee's name, a work assignment code number shown in parentheses, and the date of this assignment. The cards are to be filed according to the following rules:

First: File in alphabetical order
Second: When two or more cards have the same employee's name, file according to the work assignment number beginning with the lowest number.
Third: When two or more cards have the same employee's name and same assignment number, file according to the assignment date beginning with the earliest date.

Column II shows the cards arranged in four different orders. Pick the answer (A, B, C, or D) in Column II which shows the cards arranged according to the above filing rules.

SAMPLE QUESTION: See Sample Question (with answer) for Test 4.

Now answer the following questions according to these rules.

COLUMN I

1. 1. Prichard   (013469)   4/6/21
    2. Parks   (678941)   2/7/21
    3. Williams   (551467)   3/6/20
    4. Wilson   (551466)   8/9/17
    5. Stanhope   (300014)   8/9/17

COLUMN II
A. 5, 4, 3, 2, 1
B. 1, 2, 5, 3, 4
C. 2, 1, 5, 3, 4
D. 1, 5, 4, 3, 2

1.____

2. 1. Ridgeway   (623809)   8/11/21
    2. Travers   (305439)   4/5/17
    3. Tayler   (818134)   7/5/18
    4. Travers   (305349)   5/6/20
    5. Ridgeway   (623089)   10/9/21

A. 5, 1, 3, 4, 2
B. 5, 1, 3, 2, 4
C. 1, 5, 3, 2, 4
D. 1, 5, 4, 2, 3

2.____

3. 1. Jaffe   (384737)   2/19/21
    2. Inez   (859176)   8/8/22
    3. Ingrahm   (946460)   8/6/19
    4. Karp   (256146)   5/5/20
    5. Ingrahm   (946460)   6/4/20

A. 3, 5, 2, 4, 1
B. 3, 5, 2, 1, 4
C. 2, 3, 5, 1, 4
D. 2, 3, 5. 4, 1

3.____

4. 1. Marrano   (369421)   7/24/19
    2. Marks   (652910)   2/23/21
    3. Netto   (556772)   3/10/21
    4. Marks   (652901)   2/17/22
    5. Netto   (556772)   6/17/20

A. 1, 5, 3, 4, 2
B. 3, 5, 4, 2, 1
C. 2, 4, 1, 5, 3
D. 4, 2, 1, 5, 3

4.____

2 (#5)

	COLUMN I			COLUMN II	
5.	1. Abernathy	(712467)	6/23/20	A. 5, 3, 1, 2, 4	5.____
	2. Acevedo	(680262)	6/23/18	B. 5, 4, 2, 3, 1	
	3. Aaron	(967647)	1/17/19	C. 1, 3, 5, 2, 4	
	4. Acevedo	(680622)	5/14/17	D. 2, 4, 1, 5, 3	
	5. Aaron	(967647)	4/1/15		
6.	1. Simon	(645219)	8/19/20	A. 4, 1, 2, 5, 3	6.____
	2. Simon	(645219)	9/2/18	B. 4, 5, 2, 1, 3	
	3. Simons	(645218)	7/7/20	C. 3, 5, 2, 1, 4	
	4. Simms	(646439)	10/12/21	D. 5, 1, 2, 3, 4	
	5. Simon	(645219)	10/16/17		
7.	1. Rappaport	(312230)	6/11/21	A. 4, 3, 1, 2, 5	7.____
	2. Rascio	(777510)	2/9/20	B. 4, 3, 1, 5, 2	
	3. Rappaport	(312230)	7/3/17	C. 3, 4, 1, 5, 2	
	4. Rapaport	(312330)	9/6/20	D. 5, 2, 4, 3, 1	
	5. Rascio	(777501)	7/7/20		
8.	1. Johnson	(843250)	6/8/17	A. 1, 3, 2, 4, 5	8.____
	2. Johnson	(843205)	4/3/20	B. 1, 3, 2, 5, 4	
	3. Johnson	(843205)	8/6/17	C. 3, 2, 1, 4, 5	
	4. Johnson	(843602)	3/8/21	D. 3, 2, 1, 5, 4	
	5. Johnson	(843602)	8/3/20		

KEY (CORRECT ANSWERS)

1.	C	5	A
2.	A	6.	B
3.	C	7.	B
4.	D	8.	D

TEST 6

DIRECTIONS: In each of the following questions there are four groups of names. One of the groups in each question is NOT in correct alphabetic order. Mark the letter of that group next to the number that corresponds to the number of the question.

1. A. Ace Advertising Agency; Acel, Erwin; Ad Graphics; Ade, E.J. & Co.
   B. Advertising Bureau, Inc.; Advertising Guild, Inc.; Advertising Ideas, Inc.; Advertising Sales Co.
   C. Allan Associates; Allen-Wayne, Inc.; Alley & Richards, Inc.; Allum, Ralph
   D. Anderson & Cairnes; Amos Parrish & Co.; Anderson Merrill Co.; Anderson, Milton

   1.____

2. A. Bach, Henry; Badillo, John; Baer, Budd; Bair, Albert
   B. Baker, Lynn; Bakers, Albert; Bailin, Henry; Bakers Franchise Corp.
   C. Bernhardt, Manfred; Bernstein, Jerome; Best, Frank; Benton Associates
   D. Brandford, Edward; Branstatter Associates; Brown, Martel; Browne, Bert

   2.____

3. A. Cone, Robert; Contempo, Bernard; Conti Advertising; Cooper, James
   B. Cramer, Zed; Creative Sales; Crofton, Ada; Cromwell, Samuel
   C. Cheever, Fred; Chernow Advertising; Chenault Associates; Chester, Arthur
   D. Chain Store Advertising; Chair Lawrence & Co.; Chaite, Alexander E.; Chase, Luis

   3.____

4. A. Delahanty, Francis; Dela McCarthy Associates; Delehanty, Kurnit; Delroy, Stewart
   B. Doerfler, B.R.; Doherty, Clifford; Dorchester Apartments; Dorchester, Monroe
   C. Drayer, Stella; Dreher, Norton; Dreyer, Harvey; Dryer, Lester
   D. Duble, Normal; Duevell, William C.; Du Fine, August; Dugan, Harold

   4.____

5. A. Esmond, Walter; Esty, Willia; Ettinger, Carl; Everett, Austin
   B. Enlos, Cartez; Entertainment, Inc.; Englemore, Irwin; Equity Associates
   C. Einhorn, Anna Mrs.; Einhorn, Arlene; Eisele, Mary; Eisele, Minnie Mrs.
   D. Eagen, Roy; Egale, George; Egan, Barrett; Eisen, Henry

   5.____

6. A. Funt, Rand Inc.; Furman, Fainer & Co.; Furman Roth & Co.; Fusco, Frank A.
   B. Friedan, Phillip; Friedman, Mitchell; Friend, Harvey; Friend, Herbert
   C. Folkart Greeting Cards; Food Service; Foote, Cornelius; Foreign Advertising
   D. Finkels, Eliot; Finnerman, John; Finneran, Joseph; Firestone, Albert

   6.____

7. A. Gubitz, Jay; Guild, Dorothy; Gumbiner, B.; Gussow, Leonard
   B. Gore, Smith; Gotham Art, Inc.; Gotham Editors Service; Gotham-Vladimir, Inc.
   C. Georgian, Wolf; Gerdts, H.J.; German News Co.; Germaine, Werner
   D. Gardner, Fred; Gardner, Roy; Garner, Roy; Gaynor & Ducal Inc.

   7.____

2 (#6)

8. A. Howard, E. T.; Howard, Francis; Howson, Allen; Hoyt, Charles
    B. Houston, Byron; House of Graphics; Rowland, Lynne; Hoyle, Mortimer
    C. Hi-Lite Art Service; Hickerson, J.M.; Hickey, Murphy; Hicks; Gilbert
    D. Hyman, Bram; Hyman, Charles B.; Hyman, Claire; Hyman, Claude

8._____

9. A. Idone, Leopold; Ingraham, Evelyn; Ianuzzi, Frank; Itkin, Simon
    B. Ideas, Inc.; Inter-Racial Press, Inc.; International Association; Iverson, Ford
    C. Il Trionofo; Inwood Bake Shop; Iridor, Rose; Italian Pastry
    D. Ionadi, Anthony Irena, Louise; Iris, Ysabella; Isabelle, Arlia

9._____

10. A. Jonas, Myron; Johnstone, John; Jones, Julius; Joptha, Meyer
    B. Jeanne's Beauty Shoppe; Jeger, Jans; Jem, H.; Jim's Grill
    C. Jacobs, Abraham & Co., Jacobs, Harold A.; Jacobs, Joseph; Jacobs, M.J.
    D. Japan Air Lines; Jensen, Arne; Judson, P.; Juliano, Jeremiah

10._____

KEY (CORRECT ANSWERS)

1.	D	6.	D
2.	B	7.	C
3.	C	8.	B
4.	A	9.	A
5.	B	10.	A

TEST 7

DIRECTIONS: Below are ten groups of names, numbered 1 through 10. For each group, three different filing arrangements of the names in the group are given. In only ONE of these arrangements are the names in correct filing order according to standard rules for filing. For each group, select the ONE arrangement, lettered A, B, C, that is CORRECT.

1. Arrangement A
Nichols, C. Arnold
Nichols, Bruce
Nicholson, Arthur

   Arrangement B
Nichols, Bruce
Nichols, C. Arnold
Nicholson, Arthur

   Arrangement C
Nicholson, Arthur
Nichols, Bruce
Nichols, C. Arnold

   1.____

2. Arrangement A
Schaefer's Drug Store
Schaefer, Harry T.
Schaefer Bros.

   Arrangement B
Schaefer Bros.
Schaefer, Harry T.
Schaefer's Drug Store

   Arrangement C
Schaefer Bros.
Schaefer's Drug Store
Schaefer, Harry T.

   2.____

3. Arrangement A
Adams' Dime Store
Adami, David
Adams, Donald

   Arrangement B
Adami, David
Adams' Dime Store
Adams, Donald

   Arrangement C
Adami, David
Adams. Donald
Adams' Dime Store

   3.____

4. Arrangement A
Newton, Jas. F.
Newton, Janet
Newton-Jarvis Law Firm

   Arrangement B
Newton-Jarvis Law Firm
Newton, Jas. F.
Newton, Janet

   Arrangement C
Newton, Janet
Newton-Jarvis Law Firm
Newton, Jas. F.

   4.____

5. Arrangement A
Radford and Bigelow
Radford Transfer Co.
Radford-Smith, Albert

   Arrangement B
Radford and Bigelow
Radford-Smith, Albert
Radford Transfer Co.

   Arrangement C
Radford Transfer Co.
Radford and Bigelow
Radford-Smith, Albert

   5.____

6. Arrangement A
Trent, Inc.
Trent Farm Products
20th Century Film Corp.

   Arrangement B
20th Century Film Corp.
Trent Farm Products
Trent, Inc.

   Arrangement C
Trent Farm Products
Trent, Inc.
20th Century Film Corp.

   6.____

7. Arrangement A
Morrell, Ralph
M.R.B. Paper Co.
Mt. Ranier Hospital

   Arrangement B
Morrell, Ralph
Mt. Ranier Hospital
M.R.B. Paper Co.

   Arrangement C
M.R.B. Paper Co.
Morrell, Ralph
Mt. Ranier Hospital

   7.____

8. Arrangement A
Vanity Faire Shop
Van Loon, Charles
The Williams Magazine Corp.

   Arrangement B
The Williams Magazine Corp.
Van Loon, Charles
Vanity Faire Shop

   Arrangement C
Van Loon, Charles
Vanity Faire Shop

   8.____

9. Arrangement A
   Crane and Jones Ins. Co.
   Little Folks Shop
   L.J. Coughtry Mfg. Co.

   Arrangement B
   L.J. Coughtry Mfg. Co.
   Crane and Jones Ins. Co.
   Little Folks Shop

   Arrangement C
   Little Folks Shop
   L.J. Coughtry Mfg. Co.
   Crane and Jones Ins. Co.

   9.____

10. Arrangement A
    South Arlington Garage
    N.Y. State Dept. of Audit and Control
    State Antique Shop

    Arrangement B
    N.Y. State Dept. of Audit and Control
    South Arlington Garage
    State Antique Shop

    Arrangement C
    State Antique Shop
    South Arlington Garage
    N.Y. State Dept. of Audit and Control

    10.____

KEY (CORRECT ANSWERS)

1.	B	6.	C
2.	C	7.	A
3.	B	8.	A
4.	A	9.	B
5.	B	10.	B

TEST 8

DIRECTIONS: Below are ten groups of names, numbered 1 through 10. For each group, three different filing arrangements of the names in the group are given. In only ONE of these arrangements are the names in correct filing order according to standard rules for filing. For each group, select the ONE arrangement, lettered A, B, C, that is CORRECT.

1. Arrangement A
   Gillilan, William
   Gililane, Ethel
   Gillihane, Harry

   Arrangement B
   Gililane, Ethel
   Gillihane, Harry
   Gillilan, William

   Arrangement C
   Gillihane, Harry
   Gillilan, William
   Gililane, Ethel

   1.____

2. Arrangement A
   Stevens, J. Donald
   Stevenson, David
   Stevens, James

   Arrangement B
   Stevenson, David
   Stevens, J. Donald
   Stevens, James

   Arrangement C
   Stevens, J. Donald
   Stevens, James
   Stevenson, David

   2.____

3. Arrangement A
   Brooks, Arthur E.
   Brooks, H. Albert
   Brooks, H.T.

   Arrangement B
   Brooks, H.T.
   Brooks, H. Albert
   Brooks, Arthur E.

   Arrangement C
   Brooks, H. Albert
   Brooks, Arthur E.
   Brooks, H.T.

   3.____

4. Arrangement A
   Lafayette, Earl
   Le Grange, Wm. J.
   La Roux Haberdashery

   Arrangement B
   Le Grange, Wm. J.
   La Roux Haberdashery
   Lafayette, Earl

   Arrangement C
   Lafayette, Earl
   La Roux Haberdashery
   Le Grange, Wm. J.

   4.____

5. Arrangement A
   Mosher Bros.
   Mosher's Auto Repair
   Mosher, Dorothy

   Arrangement B
   Mosher's Auto Repair
   Mosher Bros.
   Mosher, Dorothy

   Arrangement C
   Mosher Bros.
   Mosher, Dorothy
   Mosher's Auto Repair

   5.____

6. Arrangement A
   Ainsworth, Inc.
   Ainsworth, George
   Air-O-Pad Co.

   Arrangement B
   Ainsworth, George
   Ainsworth, Inc.
   Air-O-Pad Co.

   Arrangement C
   Air-O-Pad Co.
   Ainsworth, George
   Ainsworth, Inc.

   6.____

7. Arrangement A
   Peters' Printing Co.
   Peerbridge, Alfred
   Peters, Paul

   Arrangement B
   Peterbridge, Alfred
   Peters, Paul
   Petters' Printing Co.

   Arrangement C
   Peters, Paul
   Peters' Printing Co.
   Peterbridge, Alfred

   7.____

8. Arrangement A
   Sprague-Miller, Elia
   Sprague (and) Reed
   Sprague Insurance Co.

   Arrangement B
   Sprague (and) Reed
   Sprague Insurance Co.
   Sprague-Miller, Ella

   Arrangement C
   Sprague Insurance Co.
   Sprague (and) Reed
   Sprague-Miller, Ella

   8.____

2 (#8)

9.
Arrangement A	Arrangement B	Arrangement C	9._____
Ellis, Chalmers Adv. Agency	Ellis, Chas.	Ellis, Charlotte	
Ellis, Chas.	Ellis, Charlotte	Ellis, Chas.	
Ellis, Charlotte	Ellis, Chalmers Adv. Agency	Ellis, Chalmers Adv. Agency	

10.
Arrangement A	Arrangement B	Arrangement C	10._____
Adams, Paul	Five Acres Coffee Shop	Adams, Paul	
Five Acres Coffee Shop	Adams, Paul	Fielding Adjust Co.	
Fielding Adjust. Co.	Fielding Adjust. Co.	Five Acres Coffee Shop	

KEY (CORRECT ANSWERS)

1.	B	6.	B
2.	C	7.	B
3.	A	8.	C
4.	C	9.	A
5.	B	10.	C

TEST 9

DIRECTIONS: Below in Section A is a diagram representing 40 divisional drawers in alphabetic file, numbered 1 through 40. Below in Section B is a list of 30 names to be filed, numbered 1 through 30, with a drawer number opposite each name, representing the drawer in which it is assumed a file clerk has filed the name.

Determine which are filed CORRECTLY and which are filed INCORRECTLY based on standard rules for indexing and filing. If the name is filed CORRECTLY, print in the space at the right the letter C. If the name is filed INCORRECTLY, print in the space at the right the letter I.

SECTION A

1 Aa-Al	6 Bs-Bz	11 Ea-Er	16 Gp-Gz	21 Kp-Kz	26 Mo-Mz	31 Qa-Qz	36 Ta-Ti
2 Am-Au	7 Ca-Ch	12 Es-Ez	17 Ha-Hz	22 La-Le	27 Na-Nz	32 Ra-Rz	37 Tj-Tz
3 Av-Az	8 Ci-Co	13 Fa-Fr	18 Ia-Iz	23 Lf-Lz	28 Oa-Oz	33 Sa-Si	38 U-V
4 Ba-Bi	9 Cp-Cz	14 Fa-Fz	19 Ja-Jz	24 Ma-Mi	29 Pa-Pr	34 Sj-St	39 Wa-Wz
5 Bj-Br	10 Da-Dz	15 Ga-Go	20 Ka-Ko	25 Mj-Mo	30 Ps-Pz	35 Su-Sz	40 X-Y-Z

SECTION B

	Name or Title	Drawer No.	
1.	William O'Dea	28	1.____
2.	J. Arthur Crawford	8	2.____
3.	DuPont Chemical Co.	10	3.____
4.	Arnold Bros. Mfg. Co.	2	4.____
5.	Dr. Charles Ellis	10	5.____
6.	Gray and Doyle Adv. Agency	16	6.____
7.	Tom's Smoke Shop	37	7.____
8.	Wm. E. Jarrett Motor Corp.	39	8.____
9.	Penn-York Air Service	29	9.____
10.	Corinne La Fleur	13	10.____
11.	Cartright, Incorporated	7	11.____

143

2 (#9)

12.	7th Ave. Market	24	12.____
13.	Ft. Schuyler Apts.	13	13.____
14.	Madame Louise	23	14.____
15.	Commerce Dept., U.S. Govt.	38	15.____
16.	Norman Bulwer-Lytton	6	16.____
17.	Hilton Memorial Library	17	17.____
18.	The Linen Chest Gift Shop	36	18.____
19.	Ready Mix Supply Co.	32	19.____
20.	City Service Taxi	8	20.____
21.	A.R.C. Transportation Co.	37	21.____
22.	New Jersey Insurance Co.	19	22.____
23.	Capt. Larry Keith	20	23.____
24.	Girl Scouts Council	15	24.____
25.	University of Michigan	24	25.____
26.	Sister Ursula	38	26.____
27.	Am. Legion Post #9	22	27.____
28.	Board of Hudson River Reg. Dist.	17	28.____
29.	Mid West Bus Lines	39	29.____
30.	South West Tours, Inc.	34	30.____

KEY (CORRECT ANSWERS)

1.	C	11.	C	21.	I
2.	I	12.	I	22.	I
3.	C	13.	C	23.	C
4.	C	14.	I	24.	C
5.	I	15.	C	25.	I
6.	C	16.	C	26.	I
7.	C	17.	C	27.	I
8.	I	18.	I	28.	C
9.	C	19.	C	29.	I
10.	I	20.	C	30.	C

TEST 10

DIRECTIONS: Each question or incomplete statement is followed by several suggested answers or completions. Select the one that BEST answers the question or completes the statement. *PRINT THE LETTER OF THE CORRECT ANSWER IN THE SPACE AT THE RIGHT.*

1. Of the following statements about the numeric system of filing, the one which is CORRECT is that it
   A. is the least accurate of all methods of filing
   B. eliminates the need for cross-referencing
   C. allows for very limited expansion
   D. requires a separate index

   1.____

2. When more than one name or subject is involved in a piece of correspondence to be filed, the office assistant should GENERALLY
   A. prepare a cross-reference sheet
   B. establish a geographical filing system
   C. prepare out-guides
   D. establish a separate index card for noting such correspondence

   2.____

3. A tickler file is MOST generally used for
   A. identification of material contained in a numeric file
   B. maintenance of a current listing of telephone numbers
   C. follow-up of matters requiring future attention
   D. control of records borrowed or otherwise removed from the file

   3.____

4. In filing, the name Ms. "Ann Catalana-Moss" should GENERALLY be indexed as
   A. Moss, Catalana, Ann (Ms.)
   B. Catalana-Moss, Ann (Ms.)
   C. Ann Catalana-Moss (Ms.)
   D. Moss-Catalana, Ann (Ms.)

   4.____

5. An office assistant has a set of four cards, each of which contains one of the following names.
   In alphabetic filing, the FIRST of the cards to be filed is
   A. (Ms.) Alma John
   B. Mrs. John (Patricia) Edwards
   C. John-Edward School Supplies, Inc.
   D. John H. Edwards

   5.____

6. Generally, of the following, the name to be filed FIRST in an alphabetical filing system is
   A. Diane Maestro
   B. Diana McElroy
   C. James Mackell
   D. James McKell

   6.____

2 (#10)

7. According to generally recognized rules of filing in an alphabetic filing system, the one of the following names which normally should be filed LAST is
   A. Department of Education, New York State
   B. F. B. I.
   C. Police Department of New York City
   D. P.S. 81 of New York City

7.____

KEY (CORRECT ANSWERS)

1. D
2. A
3. C
4. B
5. D
6. C
7. B

ARITHMETIC
EXAMINATION SECTION
TEST 1

DIRECTIONS: Each question or incomplete statement is followed by several suggested answers or completions. Select the one that *BEST* answers the question or completes the statement. *PRINT THE LETTER OF TEE CORRECT ANSWER IN THE SPACE AT THE RIGHT.*

1. Add $4.34, $34.50, $6.00, $101.76, $90.67. From the result, subtract $60.54 and $10,56.   1.____

   A. $76.17   B. $156.37   C. $166.17   D. $300.37

2. Add 2,200, 2,600, 252 and 47.96. From the result, subtract 202.70, 1,200, 2,150 and 434.43.   2.____

   A. 1,112.83   B. 1,213.46   C. 1,341.51   D. 1,348.91

3. Multiply 1850 by .05 and multiply 3300 by .08 and, then, add both results,   3.____

   A. 242.50   B. 264,00   C. 333.25   D. 356.50

4. Multiply 312.77 by .04. Round off the result to the nearest hundredth.   4.____

   A. 12.52   B. 12.511   C. 12.518   D. 12.51

5. Add 362.05, 91.13, 347.81 and 17.46 and then divide the result by 6. The answer, rounded off to the nearest hundredth, is: 5.____

   A. 138.409   B. 137.409   C. 136.41   D. 136.40

6. Add 66.25 and 15.06 and, then, multiply the result by 2 1/6. The answer is, most nearly,   6.____

   A. 176.18   B. 176.17   C. 162.66   D. 162.62

7. Each of the following items contains three decimals. In which case do *all* three decimals have the *SAME* value?   7.____

   A. .3; .30; .03   B. .25; .250; .2500
   C. 1.9; 1.90;1.09   D. .35; .350; .035

8. Add 1/2 the sum of (539.84 and 479.26) to 1/3 the sum of (1461.93 and 927.27). Round off the result to the nearest whole number.   8.____

   A. 3408   B. 2899   C. 1816   D. 1306

9. Multiply $5,906.09 by 15% and, then, divide the result by 3 and round off to the nearest cent.   9.____

   A. $295.30   B. $885.91   C. $2,657.74   D. $29,530.45

10. Multiply 630 by 517.   10.____

    A. 325,710   B. 345,720   C. 362,425   D. 385,660

149

11. Multiply 35 by 846.

    A. 4050   B. 9450   C. 18740   D. 29610

12. Multiply 823 by 0.05.

    A. 0.4115   B. 4.115   C. 41.15   D. 411.50

13. Multiply 1690 by 0.10.

    A. 0.169   B. .1.69   C. 16.90   D. 169.0

14. Divide 2765 by 35.

    A. 71   B. 79   C. 87   D. 93

15. From $18.55 subtract $6.80.

    A. $9.75   B. $10.95   C. $11.75   D. $25.35

16. The sum of 2.75 + 4.50 + 3.60 is:

    A. 9.75   B. 10.85   C. 11.15   D. 11.95

17. The sum of 9.63 + 11.21 + 17.25 is:

    A. 36.09   B. 38.09   C. 39.92   D. 41.22

18. The sum of 112.0 + 16.9 + 3.84 is:

    A. 129.3   B. 132.74   C. 136.48   D. 167.3

19. When 65 is added to the result of 14 multiplied by 13, the answer is:

    A. 92   B. 182   C. 247   D. 16055

20. From $391.55 subtract $273.45.

    A. $118.10   B. $128.20   C. $178.10   D. $218.20

KEY (CORRECT ANSWERS)

1.	C	11.	D
2.	A	12.	C
3.	D	13.	D
4.	D	14.	B
5.	C	15.	C
6.	B	16.	B
7.	B	17.	B
8.	D	18.	B
9.	C	19.	C
10.	A	20.	A

SOLUTIONS TO PROBLEMS

1. ($4.34 + $34.50 + $6.00 + $101.76 + $90.67) - ($60.54 + $10.56) = $237.27 - $71.10 = $166.17.

2. (2200 + 2600 + 252 + 47.96) - (202.70 + 1200 + 2150 + 434.43) = 5099.96 - 3987.13 = 1112.83

3. (1850)(.05) + (3300)(.08) = 92.5 + 264 = 356.50

4. (312.77)(.04) = 12.5108 = 12.51 to nearest hundredth

5. $(362.05+91.13+347.81+17.46) \div 6 = 136.40\overline{83} = 136.41$ to nearest hundredth

6. $(66.25+15.06)(2\frac{1}{6}) = 176.17\overline{16} \approx 176.17$

7. .25 = .250 = .2500

8. $(\frac{1}{2})(539.84+479.26) + \frac{1}{3}(1461.93+927.27)$ = 509.55 + 796.4 = 1305.95 = 1306 nearest whole number

9. ($5906.09)(.15) ÷ 3 = ($885.9135)/3 = 295.3045 = $295.30 to nearest cent

10. (630)(517) = 325,710

11. (35)(846) = 29,610

12. (823)(.05) = 41.15

13. (1690)(10) = 169.0

14. 2765÷3.5 = 79

15. $18.55 - $6.80 = $11.75

16. 2.75 + 4.50 + 3.60 = 10.85

17. 9.63 + 11.21 + 17.25 = 38.09

18. 112.0 + 16.9 + 3.84 = 132.74

19. 65 + (14)(13) = 65 + 182 = 247

20. $391.55 - $273.45 = $118.10

TEST 2

DIRECTIONS Each question or incomplete statement is followed by several suggested answers or completions. Select the one that *BEST* answers the question or completes the statement. *PRINT THE LETTER OF TEE CORRECT ANSWER IN THE SPACE AT THE RIGHT.*

1. The sum of $29.61 + $101.53 + $943.64 is: 1.____
   A. $983.88   B. $1074.78   C. $1174.98   D. $1341.42

2. The sum of $132.25 + $85.63 + $7056,44 is: 2.____
   A. $1694.19   B. $7274.32   C. $8464.57   D. $9346.22

3. The sum of 4010 + 1271 + 838 + 23 is: 3.____
   A. 6142   B. 6162   C. 6242   D. 6362

4. The sum of 53632 + 27403 + 98765 + 75424 is: 4.____
   A. 19214   B. 215214   C. 235224   D. 255224

5. The sum of 76342 + 49050 + 21206 + 59989 is: 5.____
   A. 196586   B. 206087   C. 206587   D. 234487

6. The sum of $452.13 + $963.45 + $621.25 is: 6.____
   A. $1936.83   B. $2036.83   C. $2095.73   D. $2135.73

7. The sum of 36392 + 42156 + 98765 is: 7.____
   A. 167214   B. 177203   C. 177313   D. 178213

8. The sum of 40125 + 87123 + 24689 is: 8.____
   A. 141827   B. 151827   C. 151937   D. 161947

9. The sum of 2379 + 4015 + 6521 + 9986 is: 9.____
   A. 22901   B. 22819   C. 21801   D. 21791

10. From 50962 subtract 36197. 10.____
    A. 14675   B. 14765   C. 14865   D. 24765

11. From 90000 subtract 31928. 11.____
    A. 58072   B. 59062   C. 68172   D. 69182

12. From 63764 subtract 21548. 12.____
    A. 42216   B. 43122   C. 45126   D. 85312

13. From $9605.13 subtract $2715.96. 13.____
    A. $12,321.09   B. $8,690.16   C. $6,990.07   D. $6,889.17

14. From 76421 subtract 73101.

    A. 3642   B. 3540   C. 3320   D. 3242

15. From $8.25 subtract $6.50.

    A. $1.25   B. $1.50   C. $1.75   D. $2.25

16. Multiply 583 by 0.50.

    A. $291.50   B. 28.15   C. 2.815   D. 0.2815

17. Multiply 0.35 by 1045.

    A. 0.36575   B. 3.6575   C. 36.575   D. 365.75

18. Multiply 25 by 2513.

    A. 62825   B. 62725   C. 60825   D. 52825

19. Multiply 423 by 0.01.

    A. 0.0423   B. 0.423   C. 4.23   D. 42.3

20. Multiply 6.70 by 3.2.

    A. 2.1440   B. 21.440   C. 214.40   D. 2144.0

KEY (CORRECT ANSWERS)

1. B
2. B
3. A
4. D
5. C

6. B
7. C
8. C
9. A
10. B

11. A
12. A
13. D
14. C
15. C

16. A
17. D
18. A
19. C
20. B

SOLUTIONS TO PROBLEMS

1. $29.61 + $101.53 + $943.64 = $1074.78

2. $132.25 + $85.63 + $7056.44 = $7274.32

3. 4010 + 1271 + 838 + 23 = 6142

4. 53,632 + 27,403 + 98,765 + 75,424 = 255,224

5. 76,342 + 49,050 + 21,206 + 59,989 = 206,587

6. $452.13 + $963.45 + $621.25 = $2036.83

7. 36,392 + 42,156 + 98,765 = 177,313

8. 40,125 + 87,123 + 24,689 = 151,937

9. 2379 + 4015 + 6521 + 9986 = 22,901

10. 50962 - 36197 = 14,765

11. 90,000 - 31,928 = 58,072

12. 63,764 - 21,548 = 42,216

13. $9605.13 - $2715.96 = $6889.17

14. 76,421 - 73,101 = 3320

15. $8.25 - $6.50 = $1.75

16. (583)(.50) = 291.50

17. (.35)(1045) = 365.75

18. (25)(2513) = 62,825

19. (423)(.01) = 4.23

20. (6.70)(3.2) = 21.44

TEST 3

DIRECTIONS: Each question or incomplete statement is followed by several suggested answers or completions. Select the one that *BEST* answers the question or completes the statement. *PRINT THE LETTER OF TEE CORRECT ANSWER IN THE SPACE AT THE RIGHT.*

Questions 1-4.

DIRECTIONS: For each of Questions 1-4, perform the indicated arithmetic and choose the correct answer from among the four choices given.

1. 12.485
   + 347

   A. 12,038   B. 12,128   C. 12,782   D. 12,832

   1._____

2. 74,137
   + 711

   A. 74,326   B. 74,848   C. 78,028   D. .D. 78,926

   2._____

3. 3,749
   - 671

   A. 3,078   B. 3,168   C. 4,028   D. 4,420

   3._____

4. 19,805
   -18904

   A. 109   B. 901   C. 1,109   D. 1,901

   4._____

5. When 119 is subtracted from the sum of 2016 + 1634, the remainder is:

   A. 2460   B. 3531   C. 3650   D. 3769

   5._____

6. Multiply 35 X 65 X 15.

   A. 2275   B. 24265   C. 31145   D. 34125

   6._____

7. 90% expressed as a decimal is:

   A. .009   B. .09   C. .9   D. 9.0

   7._____

8. Seven-tenths of a foot expressed in inches is:

   A. 5.5   B. 6.5   C. 7   D. 8.4

   8._____

9. If 95 men were divided into crews of five men each, the *number* of crews that will be formed is:

   A. 16   B. 17   C. 18   D. 19

   9._____

155

2 (#3)

10. If a man earns $19.50 an hour, the *number* of working hours it will take him to earn $4,875 is, most nearly,

    A. 225   B. 250   C. 275   D. 300

11. If 5 1/2 loads of gravel cost $55.00, then 6 1/2 loads will cost:

    A. $60.   B. $62.50   C. $65.   D. $66.00

12. At $2.50 a yard, 27 yards of concrete will cost:

    A. $36.   B. $41.80   C. $54.   D. $67.50

13. A distance is measured and found to be 52.23 feet. In feet and inches, this distance is, most nearly, 52 feet *and*

    A. 2 3/4"   B. 3 1/4"   C. 3 3/4"   D. 4 1/4"

14. If a maintainer gets $5.20 per hour and time and one-half for working over 40 hours, his *gross* salary for a week in which he worked 43 hours would be

    A. $208.00   B. $223.60   C. $231.40   D. $335.40

15. The circumference of a circle is given by the formula $C = \Pi D$, where C is the circumference, D is the diameter, and Π is about 3 1/7.
    If a coil is 15 turns of steel cable has an average diameter of 20 inches, the *total* length of cable on the coil is *nearest to*

    A. 5 feet   B. 78 feet   C. 550 feet   D. 943 feet

16. The measurements of a poured concrete foundation show that 54 cubic feet of concrete have been placed.
    If payment for this concrete is to be on the basis of cubic yards, the 54 cubic feet must be

    A. multiplied by 27   B. multiplied by 3
    C. divided by 27   D. divided by 3

17. If the cost of 4 1/2 tons of structural steel is $1,800, then the cost of 12 tons is, most nearly,

    A. $4,800   B. $5,400   C. $7,200   D. $216,000

18. An hourly-paid employee working 12:00 midnight to 8:00 a.m. is directed to report to the medical staff for a physical examination at 11:00 a.m. of the same day.
    The pay allowed him for reporting will be an extra

    A. 1 hour   B. 2 hours   C. 3 hours   D. 4 hours

19. The *total* length of four pieces of 2" pipe, whose lengths are 7' 3 1/2", 4' 2 3/16", 5' 7 5/16", and 8' 5 7/8", respectively, is:

    A. 24' 6 3/4"   B. 24' 7 15/16"
    C. 25' 5 13/16"   D. 25' 6 7/8"

20. As a senior mortuary caretaker, you are preparing a monthly report, using the following figures: 20.____

    No. of bodies received   983
    No. of bodies claimed   720
    No. of bodies sent to city cemetery   14
    No. of bodies sent to medical schools   9

How many bodies remained at the end of the monthly reporting period?

  A. 230   B. 240   C. 250   D. 260

KEY (CORRECT ANSWERS)

1.	D	11.	C
2.	B	12.	D
3.	A	13.	A
4.	B	14.	C
5.	B	15.	B
6.	D	16.	C
7.	C	17.	A
8.	D	18.	C
9.	D	19.	D
10.	B	20.	B

SOLUTIONS TO PROBLEMS

1. $12{,}485 + 347 = 12{,}832$

2. $74{,}137 + 711 = 74{,}848$

3. $3749 - 671 = 3078$

4. $19{,}805 - 18{,}904 = 901$

5. $(2016 + 1634) - 119 = 3650 - 119 = 3531$

6. $(35)(65)(15) = 34{,}125$

7. $90\% = .90$ or $.9$

8. $(\frac{7}{10})(12) = 8.4$ inches

9. $95 \div 5 = 19$ crews

10. $\$4875 \div \$19.50 = 250$ days

11. Let x = cost. Then, $\dfrac{5\frac{1}{2}}{6\frac{1}{2}} = \dfrac{\$55.00}{x}$. $5\frac{1}{2} = 357.50$. Solving, $x = \$65$

12. $(\$2.50)(27) = \$67.50$

13. $.23\text{-ft.} = 2.76\text{in.}$, so $52.23\text{ft} \approx 52\,\text{ft.}\,2\frac{3}{4}\text{in.}$ ($.76 \approx \frac{3}{4}$)

14. Salary = $(\$5.20)(40) + (\$7.80)(3) = \$231.40$

15. Length $\approx (15)(3\frac{1}{7})(20) \approx 943$ in. ≈ 78 ft.

16. There are 27 cu.ft. in 1 cu.yd. To change from 54 cu.ft. to cu.yds., divide by 27.

17. $\$1800 \div 4\frac{1}{2} = = \$400$ per ton. Then, 12 tons cost $(\$400)(12) = \$4800$

18. Instead of working 12 to 8, he will be staying until 11 AM, an extra 3 hours.

19. $7'3\frac{1}{2}" + 4'2\frac{3}{16}" + 5'7\frac{5}{16}" + 8'5\frac{7}{8}" = 24'17\frac{30}{16}" = 24'18\frac{7}{8}"$

20. $983 - 720 - 14 - 9 = 240$ bodies left.

ARITHMETICAL REASONING
EXAMINATION SECTION
TEST 1

DIRECTIONS: Each question or incomplete statement is followed by several suggested answers or completions. Select the one that BEST answers the question or completes the statement. *PRINT THE LETTER OF THE CORRECT ANSWER IN THE SPACE AT THE RIGHT.*

1. Liquid toilet soap is supplied in 5-gallon cans. If each of the twelve toilet rooms in your building uses an average of one quart of toilet soap per month, the amount of cans you should be required to requisite to cover needs for a three month period is

   A. two B. three C. four D. five

   1.____

2. A corridor is ten feet wide and 210 feet long. If it takes a two-man crew about one hour to mop 5,000 square feet, the amount of time required for mopping the corridor is MOST NEARLY _____ minutes.

   A. 30
   C. 15
   B. 25
   D. 10

   2.____

3. If 75 crates of food were ordered and 100 crates were delivered, then the shipment is larger than the number ordered by _____ crates.

   A. 10 B. 15 C. 25 D. 35

   3.____

4. If 200 boxes of merchandise were ordered and 100 boxes are delivered, then the shipment is short by _____ boxes.

   A. 50 B. 100 C. 150 D. 175

   4.____

5. You are to load a hand truck with cartons weighing a total of 200 pounds. If each carton weighs 20 pounds, then the TOTAL number of cartons to be loaded is

   A. 8 B. 9 C. 10 D. 11

   5.____

6. You are to unpack twelve cartons of paper and place the paper on a storage shelf. If each carton has eight packs of paper, then the number of packs of paper that you will place on the shelf is

   A. 72 B. 84 C. 96 D. 108

   6.____

7. If floor wax costs $2.90 a gallon, then the TOTAL cost of a carton in which there are six gallons of wax is

   A. $17.40 B. $19.00 C. $21.40 D. $29.00

   7.____

8. You know that a storage shelf unit can safely hold items up to a total weight of 300 pounds. If there are already 8 boxes of canned food on the shelves of the unit, all exactly the same, and each box weighs 25 pounds, then the number of the same boxes of canned food that you can safely add to those on the shelves is

   A. 4 B. 5 C. 6 D. 7

   8.____

9. During the month of June, 40,587 people attended a city-owned swimming pool. In July, 13,014 more people attended the swimming pool than the number that had attended in June. In August, 39,655 people attended the swimming pool. The TOTAL number of people who attended the swimming pool during the months of June, July, and August was

   A. 80,242   B. 93,256   C. 133,843   D. 210,382

10. Assume that your agency has been given $2,025 to purchase file cabinets.
    If each file cabinet costs $135, how many file cabinets can your agency purchase?

    A. 8   B. 10   C. 15   D. 16

11. Assume that your unit ordered 14 staplers at a total cost of $30.20, and each stapler cost the same.
    The cost of one stapler was MOST NEARLY

    A. $1.02   B. $1.61   C. $2.16   D. $2.26

12. Assume that you are responsible for counting and recording licensing fees collected by your department. On a particular day, your department collected in fees 40 checks in the amount of $6 each, 80 checks in the amount of $4 each, 45 twenty dollar bills, 30 ten dollar bills, 42 five dollar bills, and 186 one dollar bills.
    The TOTAL amount in fees collected on that day was

    A. $1,406   B. $1,706   C. $2,156   D. $2,356

13. Assume that you are responsible for your agency's petty cash fund. During the month of February, you pay out 7 subway fares at 50¢ each and one taxi fare for $2.85. You pay out nothing else from the fund. At the end of February, you count the money left in the fund and find 3 one dollar bills, 4 quarters, 5 dimes, and 4 nickels. The amount of money you had available in the petty cash fund at the BEGINNING of February was

    A. $4.70   B. $6.35   C. $7.55   D. $11.05

14. Assume that you are assigned to sell tickets at a city-owned ice skating rink. An adult ticket costs $1.50, and a children's ticket costs $.75. At the end of a day, you find that you have sold 36 adult tickets and 80 children's tickets.
    The TOTAL amount of money you collected for that day was

    A. $81.60   B. $106.00   C. $114.00   D. $116.00

15. If each office worker files 487 index cards in one hour, how many cards can 26 office workers file in one hour?

    A. 10,662   B. 12,175   C. 12,662   D. 14,266

16. Assume a city agency has 775 office workers.
    If 2 out of 25 office workers were absent on a particular day, how many office workers reported to work on that day?

    A. 713   B. 744   C. 750   D. 773

17. If a worker earns $9.18 per hour and works a 40-hour week, his weekly pay will be

    A. $357.20   B. $366.20   C. $366.40   D. $367.20

18. If a stock clerk earns $13.12 per hour and works a 40-hour week, how much will she receive in two weeks?

    A. $1,049.60
    B. $1,049.80
    C. $1,050.60
    D. $1,051.60

19. A stock clerk earns $9.18 per hour when he works a 40-hour week and is paid for overtime at time and a half for all time worked over 40 hours.
    How much money for overtime should he receive if he worked a 48-hour week?

    A. $109.16   B. $109.28   C. $110.16   D. $110.36

20. The reorder quantity is reached by multiplying the average monthly usage by the lead time (in months) and adding the minimum balance. For a particular item, the lead time is 2 months, the minimum balance is 100, and the average monthly usage is 150.
    The reorder quantity for this item is

    A. 300   B. 400   C. 600   D. 1,000

21. If a job can be completed by 4 employees in 6 days, how many days will it take 6 employees working at an equal speed to do the same job?

    A. 2   B. 3   C. 3 1/2   D. 4

22. If your rate of pay is $8.00 an hour for a 40-hour work week, and in an emergency you volunteer to work your half-hour lunch period for 5 days at straight time, what will your TOTAL gross pay be at the end of the week?

    A. $340   B. $350   C. $370   D. $380

23. If the gross weight of a trailer truck with a load of ferrous scrap removed from your storage yard is 67,130 pounds and the tare weight is 24,570 pounds, what is the weight, in gross tons, of the scrap removed?

    A. 17   B. 18   C. 19   D. 21

24. You receive a requisition for 2 1/2 gross of machine screws. The number of machine screws you should dispense is

    A. 300   B. 324   C. 360   D. 400

25. A requisition for a ream of paper is a request for how many sheets of paper?

    A. 200   B. 500   C. 750   D. 1,000

KEY (CORRECT ANSWERS)

1. A
2. B
3. C
4. B
5. C

6. C
7. A
8. A
9. C
10. C

11. C
12. C
13. D
14. C
15. C

16. A
17. D
18. A
19. C
20. B

21. D
22. A
23. D
24. C
25. B

5 (#1)

SOLUTIONS TO PROBLEMS

1. (12)(1 qt.) = 12 qts. = 3 gallons per month. For 3 months, 9 gallons are needed. Since the soap is supplied in 5-gallon cans, 2 cans are required.

2. (10')(210') = 2100 sq.ft. Time required = (2100/5000) hrs. = .42 hrs. - 25 min. (Closest answer given is 30 min.)

3. 100 - 75 = 25 crates

4. 200 - 100 = 100 boxes

5. 200 20 = 10 cartons

6. (12) (8) = 96 packs of paper

7. ($2.90)(6) = $17.40

8. Maximum allowable number of boxes = 300 ÷ 25 = 12. Since there are already 8 boxes on the shelves, 4 more may be added.

9. Total number of people = 40,587 + 53,601 + 39,655 = 133,843

10. $2025 $135 = 15 file cabinets

11. $30.20 14 = $2.16 per stapler

12. (40)($6) + (80)($4) + (45)($20) + (30)($10) + (42)($5) + (186)($1) = $2156

13. (7)($.50) + (1)($2.85) + (3)($1) + (4)($.25) + (5)($.10) + (4)($.05) = $11.05

14. (36)($1.50) + (80)($.75) = $114.00

15. (26)(487) = 12,662 cards

16. 16. Since 23 out of 25 were present, this represents .92 of these workers. Then, (.92)(775) = 713

17. ($9.18)(40) = $367.20

18. ($13.12)(40)(2) = $1049.60

19. ($9.18)(40) + ($13.77)(8) = $477.36 total, but his overtime is (13.77)(8) = $110.16

20. Reorder quantity = (150)(2) + 100 = 400

21. (4)(6) = 24 employee-days. Then, 24 ÷ 6 = 4 days

22. ($8.00)(40) + ($8.00)(2.5) = $340

23. 67,130 - 24,570 = 42,560 lbs. 2,000 = 21.28 tons = 21 tons

24. (2 1/2)(144) = 360 machine screws

25. 1 ream = 500 sheets of paper

TEST 2

DIRECTIONS: Each question or incomplete statement is followed by several suggested answers or completions. Select the one that BEST answers the question or completes the statement. *PRINT THE LETTER OF THE CORRECT ANSWER IN THE SPACE AT THE RIGHT.*

1. A bin in your storeroom measuring 2' x 1.5' x 4' has a storage volume of _____ cubic feet.

    A. 12   B. 24   C. 50   D. 72

    1._____

2. A gill is equivalent to 8 fluid ounces.
   How many gills are required to fill a 5-gallon container with distilled water?

    A. 70   B. 75   C. 80   D. 85

    2._____

3. A storage space 8'6" wide and 9'6" long has an area that is CLOSEST to _____ square feet.

    A. 80   B. 81   C. 82   D. 83

    3._____

4. A drill bit has a diameter of 13/32 inch.
   Of the following, the decimal number CLOSEST to 13/32 is

    A. 0.406   B. 0.408   C. 0.410   D. 0.412

    4._____

5. If repaired units come into your storeroom in a palletized container indicating that the gross weight is 2250 pounds, then the

    A. container alone weighs 2250 pounds
    B. repaired units alone weigh 2250 pounds
    C. repaired units and palletized container weigh 2250 pounds
    D. weight of 2250 pounds is approximate

    5._____

6. You have 5 pieces of lumber. Their lengths are: 8'2", 6'4", 3'4", 5'9", and 4'5".
   What is the sum of the lengths of the 5 pieces of lumber?

    A. 26'   B. 26'9"   C. 27'10"   D. 28'

    6._____

7. A full reel of 1,000 feet of power distribution cable weighs 8,095 pounds. The cable weighs 7.6 pounds per foot. The weight of the empty reel is _____ pounds.

    A. 465   B. 480   C. 495   D. 510

    7._____

8. A crate 2' by 3' by 6' has a volume of _____ cubic yards.

    A. 6   B. 1 1/3   C. 18   D. 4

    8._____

9. Of 600 pieces received in a shipment, 50 are inspected. Of the 50, 10 are found damaged.
   If the 50 are a representative sampling, the number of items in the entire shipment LIKELY to be damaged is

    A. 50   B. 60   C. 80   D. 120

    9._____

165

10. A board having 3 square feet has how many square inches? 10.____

    A. 144   B. 288   C. 432   D. 576

11. A crate of material delivered to your storeroom has inscribed on it the words *Net Weight 250 pounds.* 11.____
    This means that the

    A. weight of 250 pounds is approximate
    B. material and crate together weigh 250 pounds
    C. material alone weighs 250 pounds
    D. crate alone weighs 250 pounds

12. A box contains an equal number of brass and copper tubes. Each brass tube weighs 4 pounds, each copper tube weighs 1 pound, and the empty box weighs 5 pounds. The total weight of the box and tubes is 200 pounds. 12.____
    The TOTAL number of tubes in the box is

    A. 39   B. 60   C. 78   D. 156

13. A caretaker received $70.00 for having worked from Monday through Friday, 9 M. to 5 P.M., with one hour a day for lunch. 13.____
    The number of hours the caretaker would have to work to earn $12.00 is

    A. 10   B. 6
    C. 70 divided by 12   D. 70 minus 12

14. If the cost of a broom went up from $4.00 to $6.00, the percent INCREASE in the original cost is 14.____

    A. 20   B. 25   C. 33 1/3   D. 50

15. The AVERAGE of the numbers 3, 5, 7, 8, 12 is 15.____

    A. 5   B. 6   C. 7   D. 8

16. The cost of 100 bags of cotton cleaning cloths, 89 pounds per bag, at 7 cents per pound, is 16.____

    A. $549.35   B. $623.00   C. $700.00   D. $890.00

17. If 5 1/2 bags of sweeping compound cost $55.00, then 6 1/2 bags would cost 17.____

    A. $60.00   B. $62.50   C. $65.00   D. $67.00

18. The cost of cleaning supplies in a project averaged $330.00 a month during the first 8 months of the year. How much can be spent each month for the last four months if the total amount that can be spent for cleaning supplies for the year is $3,880? 18.____

    A. $124.00   B. $220.00   C. $310.00   D. $330.00

19. A shelf in a supply closet can safely hold only 100 pounds. A package of paper towels weighs 2 pounds, a carton of disinfectant weighs 8 pounds, and a box of soap weighs 1 pound. There are already 6 cartons of disinfectant and 6 boxes of soap on the shelf. How many packages of towels can be SAFELY placed there? 19.____

    A. 20   B. 23   C. 25   D. 27

20. A cleaning solution is made up of 4 gallons of water, 1 pint of liquid soap, and 1 pint of ammonia.
    How many gallons of water are needed to use up a gallon of ammonia?

    A. 8   B. 16   C. 24   D. 32

21. Suppose a caretaker has 50 stair halls to clean. If he cleans 74% of them, the number of stair halls still UNCLEANED is

    A. 38   B. 26   C. 24   D. 13

22. If a man has a 12 foot piece of wood and wishes to cut it into two pieces so that one piece is twice as long as the other, the LONGER piece should be _____ feet.

    A. 7   B. 7 1/2   C. 8   D. 8 1/2

23. If fuel oil costs $1.09 9/10 per gallon, and $224 was the total cost for a tank fill-up, how many gallons were delivered?

    A. 203.82   B. 190.59   C. 217.38   D. 179.97

24. A drill bit has a diameter of 17/36". Of the following, the decimal equivalent CLOSEST to 17/36 is

    A. 0.444   B. 0.531   C. 0.473   D. 0.472

25. If cleaning solution costs $1.53 per gallon, what is the TOTAL cost of 2 cartons of cleaning solution when each carton holds 12 one-gallon jugs?

    A. $36.24   B. $36.72   C. $39.12   D. $37.92

KEY (CORRECT ANSWERS)

1. A
2. C
3. B
4. A
5. C

6. D
7. C
8. B
9. D
10. C

11. C
12. C
13. B
14. D
15. C

16. B
17. C
18. C
19. B
20. D

21. D
22. C
23. A
24. D
25. B

SOLUTIONS TO PROBLEMS

1. Volume = (21)(1.5')(4') = 12 cu.ft.

2. 5 gallons = (128)(5) = 640 fluid oz. Then, 640 8 = 80 gills

3. Area = (8'6")(9'6") = (8.5')(9.5') = 80.75 = 81 sq.ft.

4. 13/32 = .40625 = .406

5. Gross weight = combined weight of repaired units and palletized container.

6. 8'2" + 6'4" + 3'4" + 5'9" + 4'5" = 26'24" = 28'

7. Empty reel weight = 8095 - (7.6)(1000) = 495 lbs.

8. (2')(3')(6') = 36 cu.ft. = 36/27 = 1 1/2 cu.yds.

9. 10/50 = 20%. Then, (20%)(600) = 120 are likely to be damaged.

10. 3 sq.ft. = (3)(144) = 432 sq.in.

11. Net weight refers to the contents of the crate, not including the crate's weight.

12. Let x = number of brass and copper tubes together. Then, (1/2x)(4) + (1/2)(1) + 5 = 200. Simplifying, we get 2.5x = 195. Solving, x = 78

13. $70 is paid for (7)(5) = 35 hrs., which means $2 per hour. Thus, $12 is received in 12/2 = 6 hours.

14. Percent increase = ($2.00/$4.00)(100) = 50%

15. Average = (3+5+7+8+12)/5 = 35/5 = 7

16. Cost = (100)(89)($.07) = $623.00

17. $55 ÷ 5.5 = $10 per bag. Then, 6 1/2 bags cost (6 1/2)($10) = $65.00

18. Let x = amount spent during each of the last 4 months. Then, (8)($330) + 4x = $3880. Solving, x = $310.00

19. Let x = number of pkgs. of towels. Then, 2x + (6)(8) + (6)(1) = 100. Simplifying, 2x = 46. Solving, x = 23

20. Since 1 gallon = 8 pints, 1 gallon of ammonia requires (4)(8) = 32 gallons of water

21. Number of stair halls uncleaned = (.26)(50) = 13

22. Let x = longer piece, 1/2x = shorter piece. Then, x + 1/2x = 12. Solving, x = 8 ft.

23. $\$224 \div \$1.099 \approx 203.82$ gallons

24. $17/36 = .47\overline{2} \approx .472$

25. Total cost $= (2)(12)(\$1.53) = \$36.72$

TEST 3

DIRECTIONS: Each question or incomplete statement is followed by several suggested answers or completions. Select the one that BEST answers the question or completes the statement. *PRINT THE LETTER OF THE CORRECT ANSWER IN THE SPACE AT THE RIGHT.*

1. A storeroom is 100 feet long and 26 feet wide. One aisle 8 feet wide runs the length of the storeroom.
   One aisle 4 feet wide runs the width of the storeroom. If there were no other aisles, the number of square feet of usable storage space would be
   A. 1696   B. 1728   C. 2280   D. 2568

   1.____

2. A discount of 1% is given on all purchases of a certain item in quantities of 100 units or more. An additional discount of 1% is given on that portion of the purchase which exceeds 300.
   If 450 units are purchased at a list price of $6.00, the total cost is
   A. $2,619   B. $2,664   C. $2,670   D. $2,682

   2.____

3. The number of cartons measuring 3'x3'x2' which will be needed to pack 1,728 boxed items each measuring 3"x9"x6" is
   A. 9   B. 18   C. 108   D. 192

   3.____

4. A space 5 1/2 feet wide and 2 1/3 feet long has an area measured MOST NEARLY _____ square feet.
   A. 9   B. 10   C. 11   D. 12

   4.____

5. One man is able to load two 2 1/2 ton trucks in one hour. To load ten such trucks, it will take ten men _____ hour(s).
   A. 1/2   B. 1   C. 2   D. 2 1/2

   5.____

6. If the average height of the stacks in your section of the storehouse is 10', the area which will be occupied by 56,000 cubic feet of supplies, is MOST LIKELY to be
   A. 70'x80'   B. 60'x90'   C. 50'x60'   D. 560'x100'

   6.____

7. The number of cartons, each measuring two cubic feet, which can fit into a space which is 100 square feet in area and is 8' high is
   A. 50   B. 200   C. 400   D. 800

   7.____

8. When the floor area measures 200' by 200' and the maximum weight it can hold is 4,000 tons, then the safe floor load is _____ pounds per square foot.
   A. 20   B. 160   C. 200   D. 400

   8.____

9. A carton 1' x 1' x 3' measures _____ cubic yard(s).
   A. 1/3   B. 1/9   C. 3   D. 9

   9.____

10. You have received 6 cartons, each containing 60 boxes of staples, priced at $36.00 per carton.
    The price per box is

    A. $.10   B. $.60   C. $3.60   D. $6.00

11. The amount of space in cubic feet, required to store 100 boxes each, measuring 24" x 12" x 6", is

    A. 10   B. 100   C. 168   D. 1,008

12. Assume that it takes an average of 2 man-hours to stack 1 ton of certain supplies. In order to stack 30 tons, the number of men required to complete the job in ten hours is

    A. 6   B. 10   C. 15   D. 30

13. An area measures 20'x22 1/2'. The floor load is 100 lbs. per square foot.
    The total weight that can be stored in this area is MOST NEARLY _____ lbs.

    A. 450   B. 9,000   C. 22,500   D. 45,000

14. The price of a certain type of linoleum is $1.00 per square foot.
    The total cost of four pieces of 9'x12' linoleum is MOST NEARLY

    A. $105   B. $400   C. $430   D. $2,160

15. The number of board feet in a piece of lumber measuring 2" thick by 2' wide by 12' long is

    A. 12   B. 16   C. 24   D. 48

KEY (CORRECT ANSWERS)

1. B	6. A	11. B
2. B	7. C	12. A
3. A	8. C	13. D
4. D	9. B	14. C
5. A	10. B	15. D

SOLUTIONS TO PROBLEMS

1. (26-8)(100-4) = 1728 sq.ft. of usable space

2. 300 1% @ $5.94 = $1782; 150 2% @ $5.88 = $882. $1782 + $882 = $2664

3. (3' 3')(3' 9")(2' 6") = (12)(4)(4) = 192 boxes per carton Then, 1728 192 = 9 cartons

4. (5 1/4')(2 1/3') = 12 1/4 sq.ft. = 12 sq.ft.

5. One man could load 10 trucks in 5 hrs. Thus, 10 men would need 5/10 = 1/2 hr. to load these 10 trucks.

6. 56,000 ÷ 10' = 5600 sq.ft. Selection A which is 70'x80' would yield 5600 sq.ft.

7. (100)(8) = 800 cu.ft., and 800 2 = 400

8. (200')(200') = 40,000 sq.ft. Then, (4000)(2000) 40,000 = 200 lbs. per sq.ft.

9. (1')(1')(3') = 3 cu.ft. = 3/27 = 1/9 cu.yd.

10. $36.00 60 = $.60 per box

11. (100)(2')(1')(1/2') = 100 cu.ft.

12. 30 tons requires (2) (30) = 60 man-hours. Then, 60 10 = 6 men.

13. (100)(20')(22 1/2) = 45,000 lbs.

14. ($1.00)(9')(12')(4) = $432 = $430

15. Each side of board = (2')(12') = 24 sq.ft. Total area = (2) (24) = 48 sq.ft.

ARITHMETICAL REASONING
EXAMINATION SECTION
TEST 1

DIRECTIONS: Each question or incomplete statement is followed by several suggested answers or completions. Select the one that BEST answers the question or completes the statement. *PRINT THE LETTER OF THE CORRECT ANSWER IN THE SPACE AT THE RIGHT.*

1. Assume that it takes approximately 1 1/2 minutes to unload a dozen identical items from a delivery truck.
   At this speed, the amount of time it should take to unload a shipment of 876 items is, MOST NEARLY, _____ minutes.
   A. 90   B. 100   C. 110   D. 120

2. Assume that a shop clerk has received a bill of $108 for a delivery of clamps which cost $4.32 per dozen.
   How many clamps should there be in this delivery?
   A. 25   B. 36   C. 300   D. 360

3. Employee A has not used any leave time and has accumulated a total of 45 leave-days.
   How many months did it take employee A to have accumulated 45 leave-days if the accrual rate is 1 2/3 days per months?
   A. 25   B. 27   C. 29   D. 31

4. A shop clerk is notified that only 75 bolts can be supplied by Vendor A.
   If this represents 12.5% of the total requisition, then how many bolts were originally ordered?
   A. 125   B. 600   C. 700   D. 900

5. An enclosed square-shaped storage area with sides of 16 feet each has a safe-load capacity of 250 pounds per square foot.
   The MAXIMUM evenly distributed weight that can be stored in this area is _____ lbs.
   A. 1,056   B. 4,000   C. 64,000   D. 102,400

6. A clerical employee completed 70 progress reports the first week, 87 the second week, and 80 the third week.
   Assuming a 4-week month, how many progress reports must the clerk complete in the fourth week in order to attain an average of 85 progress reports per week for the month?
   A. 93   B. 103   C. 113   D. 133

2 (#1)

7. On the first of the month, Shop X received a delivery of 150 gallons of lubricating oil. During the month, the following amounts of oil were used on lubricating work each week: 30 quarts, 36 quarts, 20 quarts, and 48 quarts.
The amount of lubricating oil remaining at the end of the month was _____ gallons.
    A. 4   B. 33.5   C. 41.5   D. 116.5

7._____

8. For working a 35-hour week, Employee A earns a gross amount of $160.30. For each hour that Employee A works over 40 hours a week, he is entitled to 1 1/2 times his hourly wage rate.
If Employee A worked 9 hours on Monday, 8 hours on Tuesday, 9 hours 30 minutes on Wednesday, 9 hours 15 minutes on Thursday, and 9 hours 15 minutes on Friday, what should his gross salary be for that week?
    A. $206.10   B. $210.68   C. $217.55   D. $229.00

8._____

9. An enclosed cube-shaped storage bay has dimensions of 12 feet by 12 feet by 12 feet. Standard procedure requires that there be at least 1 foot of space between the walls, the ceiling and the stored items.
What is the MAXIMUM number of cube-shaped boxes with length, width, and height of 1 foot each that can be stored on 1-foot high pallets in this bay?
    A. 1,000   B. 1,331   C. 1,452   D. 1,728

9._____

10. Assume that two ceilings are to be painted. One ceiling measures 30 feet by 15 feet and the second 45 feet by 60 feet.
If one quart of paint will cover 60 square feet of ceiling, approximately how much paint will be required to paint the two ceilings?
    A. 6 gallons   B. 10 gallons   C. 13 gallons   D. 18 gallons

10._____

KEY (CORRECT ANSWERS)

1.	C	6.	B
2.	C	7.	D
3.	B	8.	C
4.	B	9.	A
5.	C	10.	C

SOLUTIONS TO PROBLEMS

1. $876 \div 12 = 73$. Then, $(73)(1\ 1/2) = 109.5 \approx 110$ minutes.

2. $\$108 \div \$4.32 = 25$. Then, $(25)(12) = 300$ clamps.

3. $45 \div 1\ 1/2 = 27$ months

4. $75 \div .125 = 600$ bolts

5. $(16)(16)(250) == 64,000$ pounds

6. $(85)(4) = 340$. Then, $340 - 70 - 87 - 80 = 103$ progress reports.

7. Changing every calculation to gallons, the amount of oil remaining is $150 - 7.5 - 9 - 5 - 12 = 116.5$.

8. $9 + 8 + 9.5 + 9.25 + 9.25 = 45$ hours. His gross pay will be $(\$4.58)(40) + (\$6.87)(5) = \$217.55$. (Note: To get his regular hourly wages, divide $\$160.30$ by 35.)

9. $12 - 1 - 1 = 10$. Maximum number of boxes is $(10)^3 = 1000$.

10. First ceiling contains $(30)(15) = 450$ sq.ft., whereas the second ceiling contains $(45)(60) = 2700$ sq.ft. The total sq.ft. $= 3150$. Now, $3150 \div 60 = 52.5$ quarts of paint $= 13.125$ or 13 gallons.

TEST 2

DIRECTIONS: Each question or incomplete statement is followed by several suggested answers or completions. Select the one that BEST answers the question or completes the statement. *PRINT THE LETTER OF THE CORRECT ANSWER IN THE SPACE AT THE RIGHT.*

1. A piping sketch is drawn to a scale of 1/8" = 1 foot.
   A vertical steam line measuring 3/4" on the sketch would have an actual length of _____ feet.
   A. 16   B. 22   C. 24   D. 28

   1._____

2. Three lengths of pipe 1'10", 3'2 1/2", and 5'7 1/2", respectively, are to be cut from a pipe 14'0" long.
   Allowing 1/8" for each pipe cut, the length of pipe remaining is
   A. 3'1 1/8"   B. 3'2 1/2"   C. 3'3 1/2"   D. 3'3 5/8"

   2._____

3. Assume that a steamfitter's helper earns $11.16 an hour and that he works 250 seven-hour days a year.
   His gross yearly salary will be
   A. 19,430   B. $19,530   C. $19,650   D. $19,780

   3._____

4. A pipe having an inside diameter of 3.48 inches and a wall thickness of .18 inches, will have an outside diameter of _____ inches.
   A. 3.84   B. 3.64   C. 3.57   D. 3.51

   4._____

5. A rectangular steel bar having a volume of 30 cubic inches, a width of 2 inches, and a height of 3 inches will have a length of _____ inches.
   A. 12   B. 10   C. 8   D. 5

   5._____

6. A pipe weighs 20.4 pounds per foot of length.
   The total weight of eight pieces of this pipe with each piece 20 feet in length is MOST NEARLY _____ pounds.
   A. 460   B. 1680   C. 2420   D. 3260

   6._____

7. In last year's budget, $7,500 was spent for office supplies. Of this amount, 60% was spent for paper supplies.
   If the price of paper has risen 20% over last year's price, then the amount that will be spent this year on paper supplies, assuming the same quantity will be purchased, will be
   A. $3,600   B. $5,200   C. $5,400   D. $6,000

   7._____

8. If it takes 4 painters 54 days to do a certain paint job, then the time it should take 5 painters working at the same speed to do the same job is MOST NEARLY _____ days.
   A. 3 1/2   B. 4   C. 4 1/2   D. 5

   8._____

2 (#2)

9. A foreman assigns a gang foreman to supervise a job which must be completed at the end of 7 working days. The gang foreman has 8 maintainers in his gang. At the end of 3 working days, although the work has been efficiently done, the job is only one-third completed.
In order to complete the job on time, without overtime, the gang foreman should request that he be given _____ more maintainers.
   A. 3   B. 4   C. 5   D. 6

9._____

10. One shipment of 70 shovels costs $140. A second shipment of 130 shovels costs $208.00.
The average cost per shovel for both shipments is MOST NEARLY
   A. $1.60   B. $1.75   C. $2.00   D. $2.50

10._____

KEY (CORRECT ANSWERS)

1.	D	6.	D
2.	D	7.	C
3.	B	8.	C
4.	A	9.	B
5.	D	10.	B

SOLUTIONS TO PROBLEMS

1. 3 1/2 ÷ 1/8 = 28 feet.

2. 14' − 1'10" − 3' 1/2" − 5'7 1/2" − 1/8" − 1/8" − 1/8" = 3'3 5/8"

3. (250)(7) = 1750 hours. Then, ($11.16)(1750) = $19,530

4. Outside diameter = 3.48 + .18 + .18 = 3.84 inches

5. Length is 30 ÷ 2 ÷ 3 = 5 inches

6. (20)(8) = 160 feet. Then, (160)(20.4) = 3264 ≈ 3260 pounds

7. ($7,500)(.60) = $4,500. Then, ($4,500)(1.20) = $5,400

8. Let x = required days. Since this is an inverse ratio, 4/5 = x/5 1/2. Then, 5x = 22.
   Solving, x = 4.4 ≈ 4 1/2

9. (8)(3) = 24 man-days were needed to complete 1/3 of the job.
   Since 2/3 of the job remains, the foreman will need 48 man-days for the remaining 4 days.
   This requires 12 men. Since he has 8 currently, he will need 4 more workers.

10. Average cost per shovel is ($140 + $208) ÷ (70+130) = $1.74, which is closest to $1.75.

TEST 3

DIRECTIONS: Each question or incomplete statement is followed by several suggested answers or completions. Select the one that BEST answers the question or completes the statement. *PRINT THE LETTER OF THE CORRECT ANSWER IN THE SPACE AT THE RIGHT.*

1. Assume that your warehouse received a shipment of 600 articles. A sample of 60 articles was inspected. Of this sample, one article was wholly defective and four articles were partly defective.
   On the basis of this sampling, you would expect the total number of defective articles in this shipment to be
   A. 5   B. 10   C. 40   D. 50

   1.____

2. Assume that you have been instructed to order mineral spirits as soon as the supply-on-hand falls to the level required for sixty days of issue.
   If the total amount of mineral spirits on hand is 960 gallons and you issue an average of 8 gallons of mineral spirits per day, and your warehouse works a five-day week, you will be required to order mineral spirits in _____ working days.
   A. 50   B. 60   C. 70   D. 80

   2.____

3. Assume that you work in a one-story warehouse where the total available floor space measures 175 feet by 140 feet. Of this floor space, one area measuring 35 feet by 75 feet is used for storing materials handling equipment, another area is measuring 10 feet by 21 feet is used for office space, and the remaining floor space is available for storage.
   The amount of floor space available for storage in this one-story warehouse is _____ square feet.
   A. 21,665   B. 21,875   C. 24,290   D. $24,500

   3.____

4. Assume that linoleum tiles measuring 9 inches by 9 inches are packed ten to a box and each box costs $3.50.
   The cost of buying enough linoleum tiles to cover an area measuring 15 feet by 21 feet is
   A. $98.00   B. $110.25   C. $196.00   D. $220.50

   4.____

5. The number of boxes measuring 3 inches by 3 inches by 3 inches that will fit into a carton measuring 2 feet by 4 feet is
   A. 2,048   B. 2,645   C. 7,936   D. 23,808

   5.____

6. The stock inventory card for paint, white, flat, one-gallon, has the following entries:

Date	Received	Shipped	Balance
April 12	-	25	75
April 13	50	75	
April 14	-	10	
April 15	25		
April 16			

   6.____

181

The balance on hand at the close of business on April 15 should be
A. 40   B. 45   C. 55   D. 65

7. The cost of one dozen pieces of screening, each measuring 4 feet 6 inches at $.10 per square foot is
A. $22.50   B. $25.00   C. $27.00   D. $27.60

8. Assume that it takes an average of ten man-hours to stack four tons of a particular item.
In order to stack 80 tons, the number of men required to complete the job in twenty hours is
A. 10   B. 20   C. 30   D. 40

9. Assume that you are required to relocate 5,000 reams of unboxed paper using only manual labor. The average time required for one laborer to pick 12 reams, carry them to the new location, and store them properly is ten minutes.
In order to complete this relocation task within one working day of seven hours, the MINIMUM number of laborers you should assign to this task is
A. 10   B. 15   C. 24   D. 70

10. Assume that you receive a shipment of 9 boxes of paper towels. Each box contains 6 dozen packages. Each package contains 200 paper towels. The total cost of the shipment of boxes is $64.80. The unit of issue for paper towels is the package.
The unit cost of the paper towels is
A. $.10   B. $.90   C. $1.20   D. $7.20

KEY (CORRECT ANSWERS)

1. D   6. D
2. B   7. C
3. A   8. A
4. C   9. A
5. A   10. A

3 (#3)

SOLUTIONS TO PROBLEMS

1. Solve for x: $5/60 = x/600$. Then, $x = 50$

2. $960 \div 8 = 120$ days. Then, $120 - 60 = 60$ days

3. Storage area is $(175)(140) - (35)(75) - (10)(21) = 21,665$ sq.ft.

4. $9 \times 9 = 81$ sq.in. $(81)(10) = 810$ sq.in. of tiles cost $3.50. $(15ft)(21ft) = (180)(252) = 45,360$ sq.in. Now, $45,360 \div 810 = 56$ boxes. Finally, $(56)(\$3.50) = \$196$

5. $(2ft)(4ft)(4ft) = (24\text{ in})(48\text{ in})(48\text{ in}) = 55,296$ sq.in. Then, $55,296/27 = 2048$ boxes.

6. Balance at end of April 13th is $75 + 50 - 75 = 50$
   Balance at end of April 14th is $50 + 0 - 10 = 40$
   Balance at end of April 15th is $40 + 25 - 0 = 65$

7. $(4\ 1/2)(5) = 224$ sq.ft. Then, $(22)(\$0.10) = \$2.25$ per piece. The cost of 12 pieces is $(\$2.25)(12) = \$27$

8. If 10 man-hours are needed for 4 tons, then 200 man-hours are needed for 80 tons. The number of men needed to do the job in 20 hours is $200 \div 20 = 10$

9. 7 hours = 420 minutes and $420 \div 10 = 42$.
   Then, $(42)(12) = 504$ reams transported per day for each laborer. Now, $5000 \div 504 \approx 9.92$, which gets rounded up to 10.

10. $(9)(72) = 648$ package. Then, $\$64.80 \div 648 = \$0.10$

www.ingramcontent.com/pod-product-compliance
Lightning Source LLC
Chambersburg PA
CBHW080732230426
43665CB00020B/2708